GROUP THERAPY FOR HIGH-CONFLICT DIVORCE

Group Therapy for High-Conflict Divorce: A Workbook for the 'No Kids in the Middle' Intervention Programme is an essential resource for reframing the divorce process to centre the child.

This workbook supports parents and practitioners using the No Kids in the Middle intervention programme, a multi-family approach for high-conflict divorce that aims to reduce psychosocial adjustment problems among children. Bridging the gap between therapy sessions and daily life, it offers exercises, testimonials and tips to stimulate parents to reflect on their own behaviour from a child's perspective. Alongside the core text *Group Therapy for High-Conflict Divorce* (2021), this will be a vital tool in a mediation process that aims to identify and end destructive patterns, to increase acceptance and to establish parenting plans to ensure the wellbeing of children.

This book will be of interest to parents going through divorce as well as to social workers and family therapists who are looking for practical guidance to support their clients. The variety of tools contained in this workbook supplement *Group Therapy for High-Conflict Divorce* and will aid those working through the No Kids in the Middle programme.

Erik van der Elst is a couples and family therapist and drama therapist at the Lorentzhuis, the Netherlands. Chairman of trainers at the Lorentzhuis, he specialises in working with high-conflict divorces.

Jeroen Wierstra is a couples and family therapist and systemic art therapist (drama), teacher and supervisor of systemic practices at the Lorentzhuis, the Netherlands. He specialises in working with high-conflict divorces and non-violent resistance (NVR) for parents.

Justine van Lawick is a clinical psychologist, family therapist and co-founder of the Lorentzhuis. She is a senior trainer in the Netherlands and abroad.

Margreet Visser is a clinical psychologist/psychotherapist and senior researcher at The Children's Trauma Center, the Netherlands. She specialises in working with traumatized children and their families. Her research focuses on the impact of destructive parental conflicts on children and family.

GROUP THERAPY FOR HIGH-CONFLICT DIVORCE

A WORKBOOK FOR THE 'NO KIDS IN THE MIDDLE' INTERVENTION PROGRAMME

Erik van der Elst, Jeroen Wierstra,
Justine van Lawick and Margreet Visser

LONDON AND NEW YORK

GROUP THERAPY FOR HIGH-CONFLICT DIVORCE

Designed cover image: No Kids in the Middle, 2011, Niels de Nies and Margreet Visser.

First published in English 2023
by Routledge
4 Park Square, Milton Park, Abingdon, Oxon OX14 4RN

and by Routledge
605 Third Avenue, New York, NY 10158

Routledge is an imprint of the Taylor & Francis Group, an informa business

© 2023 Erik van der Elst, Jeroen Wierstra, Justine van Lawick and Margreet Visser

Translated by Roelie Dröge-Bouwers

The right of Erik van der Elst, Jeroen Wierstra, Justine van Lawick and Margreet Visser to be identified as authors of this work has been asserted in accordance with sections 77 and 78 of the Copyright, Designs and Patents Act 1988.

All rights reserved. No part of this book may be reprinted or reproduced or utilised in any form or by any electronic, mechanical, or other means, now known or hereafter invented, including photocopying and recording, or in any information storage or retrieval system, without permission in writing from the publishers.

Trademark notice: Product or corporate names may be trademarks or registered trademarks, and are used only for identification and explanation without intent to infringe.

Published in Dutch by B.V. Uitgeverij SWP Amsterdam 2019

British Library Cataloguing-in-Publication Data
A catalogue record for this book is available from the British Library

ISBN: 978-0-367-53962-7 (hbk)
ISBN: 978-0-367-53961-0 (pbk)
ISBN: 978-1-003-08384-9 (ebk)

DOI: 10.4324/9781003083849

Typeset in Helvetica
by Apex CoVantage, LLC

Contents

Acknowledgments vi
Preface vii

Introduction — 1

The intake-phase: the second intake session — 9

The information evening for your social network — 10

Homework for session 1 — 11

Homework for session 2 — 12

Homework for session 3 — 23

Homework for session 4 — 39

Comprehensive chapter: escalation and de-escalation — 45

Homework for session 5 — 57

Homework for session 6 — 64

Homework for session 7 — 77

Homework for session 8 — 80

After the eighth group meeting — 90

To conclude — 92

Appendices — 95
Appendix 1 Growing up in a black-and-white world 96
Appendix 2 Growing up in a world full of stress 99
Appendix 3 Separating and letting go 101
Appendix 4 Experiences of parents from practice 103

References — 105

Acknowledgments

At this point we would like to say a few words of thanks to all colleagues of the KJTC and the Lorentzhuis who have participated in the programme so far and who have encouraged, supported and helped us to develop and compile this workbook for parents. They were the wind under our wings.

Thanks to Flora van Grinsven, Femke Valentijn and Elisabeth van der Heide. And especially Danielle Steggink, who made an important contribution to the book by taking care of the appendices about growing up in a black-and-white world full of stress. Thank you so much.

We thank Ellen Volkers, secretary at the Lorentzhuis, for all the support and encouragement we received when we were through. We also like to express our thanks for the help that Evelyn Wilms offers us. She is invaluable when it comes to all organisational matters and for setting up a national platform.

Niels de Nies deserves thanks for his support in writing and editing this workbook at a first stage. His ideas and also his efforts in thinking along with us about the structure of the workbook and in thinking up creative figures and diagrams were of great value to us.

We thank Arthur Sonnen for all the work he did behind the scenes.

We would like to thank Mark Tuitert and Frénk van der Linden for their personal stories and for allowing us to include their stories in this workbook.

We would also like to thank all parents who have given us feedback on the homework assignments over the past few years. Thanks to their feedback, efforts and perseverance, we have been able to write and compile this workbook. Thanks to all the children who participated in the programme and the young people of Villa Pinedo, children have been given a voice in this workbook. Special thanks go to Arne for writing the preface.

Finally, we would like to thank our own loved ones. They have allowed us the time to work on this workbook and have supported us during the whole process.

Preface

No Kids in the Middle

Why would I do it?
To free my children, myself and my environment from a destructive pattern that absorbs all my energy. To finally get some peace and quiet.

How can I achieve that?
By gaining insight into the destructive pattern cycle, how I am caught in it myself and how I can take steps myself to get out of it, with the help of people around me.

Tip: believe that it is possible.

Dear parents,

Let me start by admitting that I am having trouble finding a tone to greet you. It feels odd to write that I am glad or happy that you are reading this preface, knowing that the situation that lead you to this preface can probably not be described as 'happy.' I was nine myself when my parents started the divorce process, and I used to say, with a laugh and a tear, that they completed the divorce when I was twelve. Yet, it feels good to know that you are now reading this; an opportunity for change. I choose to use the word *optimistic*. I am optimistic that you are reading this, and that you have signed up for No Kids in the Middle.

I regularly tell my story to a group of parents and their network who are about to follow the programme. Then I share my experiences: the proceedings that my parents went through for three years, my father's new girlfriends, how my relationship with my parents is today. Time and again I catch myself wishing that my parents had been in the same room as you. Then I could have shown them that the child that found itself in the middle of their conflict was actually very vulnerable and was affected much more by their fights than they think.

As a child, I didn't want to let this show. I love my parents very much; I wanted to be strong for them, and therefore I always put on a bold front. I never wanted to bother them, because I could see that they were having a hard time. I wanted to help them, to solve just a little bit of their quarrels. Instead, I found myself heading towards the middle of their fight, and I had become their messenger. I so badly needed my parents to break this pattern for me. To allow me to be vulnerable and to be comforted.

Today, my parents are better able to recognise this pattern and I see that they are doing their best to make it easier for me. Even after so many years, I am still very grateful to them for this. It makes me optimistic that with this workbook and the No Kids in the Middle programme, you will be handed tools to break the cycle. I am sure that you can make it easier for your children and that they, too, will be grateful for this.

Love,
Arne (25)
Hands-on expert Villa Pinedo

GROUP THERAPY FOR HIGH-CONFLICT DIVORCE

Introduction

This is the workbook for parents that is part of the No Kids in the Middle programme. No Kids in the Middle is a joint project of the Children's and Youth Trauma Centre in Haarlem (KJTC) and the Lorentzhuis (Haarlem). The project focuses on divorced parents who are fighting and their children who are suffering as a result.

We speak of divorced parents when parents do not live under one roof. They may have been married or lived together, or they may never have formed a household together.

The conflicts between the divorced parents can be about caring for and worries about the children, but also about money, holidays, family matters and other issues. Sometimes the fight is in the open and noticeable to everyone, sometimes it is more hidden, and there is little or no mutual communication.

Sometimes one (or both) of the parents expresses serious concerns about the situation with the other parent. If these concerns relate to violence, abuse and/or addiction, we will investigate whether previous social workers and referrers have adequately sorted this out. We would like to hear all truths, and we start the No Kids in the Middle programme only when both parents display good enough parenting but still distrust each other on different issues. Based on this distrust, they want to change the other person, or the situation with the other person. They are looking for a solution to that problem.

If parents always try to find a solution in the same way, they will find themselves trapped in a fixed pattern, a vicious cycle with no way out. The children grow up in a restless environment, full of conflicts. Their parents are usually aware that they should not burden the children with their problems. But even if they are kept out of the conflict as much as possible, the children feel the tension and are bothered by it. It is not uncommon for them to have complaints. These complaints are often more inwardly directed, such as anxiety, poor sleeping and little talking, and sometimes more outwardly directed, such as arguing a lot and being rebellious. Some children do not seem to be bothered by anything. They do their best to do everything right so that they can never be a reason for more difficulties, or they manage to go their own way and free themselves from the fight between the parents. Some children choose one side in the conflict between the parents and avoid contact with the other parent. They are unable to live with the two, often contradictory truths of both parents.

Parents want to take good care of their children. If they have lasting concerns about the upbringing and development of their children, they often apply for treatment by children's therapists, or they apply for youth care. This care often becomes part of the conflict too. If that is the case, the treatment of the child is not a solution, but rather makes things more difficult for the child.

DOI: 10.4324/9781003083849-1

The programme

With our programme we try to find a way out of this repetitive conflict together with the parents and the children. Since many of the conflicts have been going on for years and often started before the parents separated, it is going to be hard work. The focus of the programme is on the parents. They need to get moving in order to improve the situation in which their children grow up.

The programme has four phases:

- an intake of two interviews;
- a network meeting;
- eight group sessions of two hours;
- an evaluation with possibly a follow-up programme.

We ask parents to do everything they can to break the vicious conflict cycles. They can do so by focusing attention on their own behaviour and by stopping to blame the other one. By finding out where and how they can break this cycle themselves, parents may manage to let go of the other. This is an enormous challenge!

We work with six families at the same time: the parents in a group of six parent couples, i.e. twelve parents, and the children (four years and up) of these parents together in another group. The children benefit greatly from the contact with fellow sufferers. They all have parents who no longer live together, and who disagree on many issues and have a lot of mutual tension. Children recognise that in one another, they can understand each other and help each other. They can strengthen each other's resilience and together find ways to be less bothered by their parents' fights.

The two children's therapists in the children's group make sure that there is a safe structure in which children can share their stories and become stronger.

The children work during the project, individually or in groups, on a presentation for their parents. This presentation is about how they experience the situation in which they live. In session 6, the children show the presentations to their parents. The therapists, too, are present during the presentations. The children show only what they want to show. This can be anything, in terms of drawings, photos, film, computer animation, music, theatre, dance – everything is possible.

While the children work together in the children's group, the parents receive therapy in the parent group. During this therapy, the important themes of conflict separation are discussed and parents help each other to find new ways. Each session starts with a 'warm-up' in which all parents, children and therapists participate. Halfway through each session, there is a 15-minute break in the family room for parents and children. There they may have a drink together. The twelve parents together make sure that these fifteen minutes run smoothly and safely. After the eight sessions, there will be an evaluation together with the parents and the people around them. They will also discuss the need and desire for a follow-up programme.

Effectiveness of No Kids in the Middle

A lot of families get moving. The research we conducted in cooperation with the VU University Amsterdam shows that the No Kids in the Middle programme reduces the conflicts of parents and that the conflicts become less destructive. It also turns out that parents accept the divorce better, become more forgiving (Visser & van Lawick, 2021) towards each other and can really let go. Only then are they really divorced!

Many parents manage to reduce the conflict. Some, however, don't. For a number of parents, there is therefore a follow-up programme in which they are stimulated or supported to further reduce the conflict.

Intake

There are two intake interviews. The first interview is with the parents and is free of obligations. It is an exploratory meeting in which the therapists of the parent group thoroughly inform the parents and in which the parents can ask questions. The meeting is not meant to discuss the problems of the parents in more detail. In addition, the parents are not supposed to get into a conversation with each other during this first meeting.

The therapists explain that the programme can start only if the parents are prepared to stop all legal proceedings or to put them on hold. Lawyers remain in the background during the programme. After all, court proceedings are synonymous with conflict, with winning or losing and therefore with distrust and a lot of tension. In the group, parents work to reduce tensions and cautiously build up trust. A legal procedure would immediately undo this.

If parents want to participate in the programme and have stopped the proceedings or have put them on hold, a second intake interview will be held, together with their children. This interview will also be attended by one, sometimes two children's therapist(s). During this interview, the children will notice that their parents will both be doing their best to reduce the tension in their environment. That will give them hope. In this session, the parent therapists will talk to each of the parents separately. The children's therapists talk to the children about their situation and what they can expect in the children's group.

Safety for the children and their parents is always a point of particular interest in this programme. Parents worry about that safety, and we obviously take their concerns seriously. When it comes to safety, we want to hear all voices and all 'truths' and not just one voice. Based on what we hear, and after contact with previous care providers (if parents agree), we assess whether the programme can work out positively.

During a joint closure of the second intake interview with parents, children and all therapists, we give brief information about the network information evening.

Network

It is our experience that many people around the parents are involved with the children and the conflicts between the parents. That is why we involve them in the therapy. During the network information evening we inform them about our approach, and they can ask questions. Throughout the programme, parents receive assignments that they can do together with the people in their network. Parents can use all the support they can get.

People in the network can be new partners, grandparents or other relatives, friends, neighbours and also professionals such as therapists and guardians. Even people from the sports club! It is important that not only the parents themselves, but also the people from their network get moving in order for the children to break free from the middle.

We ask them to cooperate. They can do so by no longer accusing one of the parents. Both parents are part of their children, so in order to support the children, it is important not to demonise either of the parents (not to blame him or her for everything).

Often parents and people from their network express a concern that one of the parents is mentally ill. They wonder if this may be the cause of all the problems. However, much research has shown that parents with a psychological vulnerability can be a good parent. When parents succeed in replacing destructive patterns for constructive patterns, tensions will be reduced. And when that happens, the vulnerabilities will play a lesser role and the symptoms will diminish, both in adults and in children.

The structure of the programme

The parents have to work hard. Hence, this workbook with assignments. It is difficult to change ingrained destructive patterns in eight sessions. But when parents take an active part in all sessions and are also involved in the project and assignments at home, together with the people from their network, chances for a positive change are best.

There are eight group sessions. We conclude each session by explaining the homework for the next session. Our intention is for the people from the network around the parents to always be involved in the assignments.

Sitting together in one room can cause a lot of tension in parents. Since a high level of stress can hinder learning and change, we work on building a mutual working relationship and on increasing the feeling of safety in the first sessions. We provide information, make contact, share our vision and give assignments to do at home. We discuss how destructive communication patterns work, what the impact of these patterns is on parents and children, and how increased stress may impact mutual communication. We also talk about the influence of the social network. We hope that the parents will be able to look differently at their situation and their issues. Understanding how these different processes work can help to de-escalate the conflict. Because insight alone is not enough, we also do a lot of exercises, in which we do not yet specifically address the situations of the parents, but we do already offer the possibility to experiment with other ways of dealing with conflicts. After three sessions, we start working on issues that the parents bring up themselves. The parents also help each other to find other ways. And if they succeed in reaching a situation in which the children are no longer caught in the middle, the parents will also be freed from their destructive trap, as will the people around them. That is what we strive for.

This workbook, a bookmark

This workbook is meant to serve as a support for parents and their social network. The workbook contains a number of assignments for each meeting. They challenge parents to think about themselves and to look at themselves and their own situation through the eyes of their child, and also to do things differently. Parents are often asked to involve people from their own network. These people can help to ease the conflict and improve communication.

Everything is to support a change process. Parents will use the book differently. Some parents will find it helpful to do all the assignments and read everything, but that does not go for every parent. There is room for differences.

The workbook bridges the gap between therapy sessions and daily life, between parents and their social network. Children and a few celebrities who grew up caught between warring parents will share their thoughts and suggestions.

The following table gives an overview of the main themes of the sessions. All themes are dealt with in the different sessions of the parent group and are also reflected in the homework assignments. Following the overview, we will go through the sessions and the corresponding assignments.

Destructive patterns	**Children**	**Separating parenthood from partnership**
Recognising the destructive pattern itself	What they experience	Separated parenting
Recognising one's own part in the pattern	Resilience, vulnerability and making children stronger	More or less communication
Changing behaviour to break the destructive patterns	A peaceful and safe interspace	Parallel parenthood
Tolerating stress and frustration	**Forgiveness** (Visser & van Lawick, 2021) **and reconciliation**	**Stories and explanations**
Vulnerability cycle	Because children need it	Explain divorced parenting with a story that children can live with
Window of tolerance	Because prolonged anger and frustration makes you sick	
Escalation and de-escalation	Cherishing good memories	
Letting go	**Network**	**From black-and-white to colour**
Relating to the divorce in a different way and how it is now	Involving the people close to you, new partner, grandparents and others in your new behaviour.	Living with multiple truths
Letting go of the illusion of control		Living with greater acceptance and joy
Focusing on your own life and making the most of it	Saying friendly things about the other parent to the network and the children	

At the end of each session, we briefly reflect on the homework for the next session, and at the beginning of each session we check how things went with the assignments at home.

In writing this workbook, we have chosen to distinguish between assignments that are essential and assignments intended for greater comprehension. The latter assignments are certainly worthwhile, but optional. They are meant to give you an extra opportunity to practice. We will not come back to them in the group meetings. If an assignment is not referred to as a comprehension assignment, we assume that all parents will do the assignment.

In the text we use both 'child' and 'children' to denote any type of family, i.e. both parents with one child and parents with several children.

We hope that the assignments in this book will be of support for parents.

The book uses the following icons:

 Purpose of the homework   Comprehension

 Assignment   Example

We wish all parents a lot of inspiration, energy and perseverance.

Good luck!

GROUP THERAPY FOR HIGH-CONFLICT DIVORCE

The intake-phase

The second intake session

When you read this book, the first intake session has already taken place. You have decided to participate in the programme. You and your children have been invited to the second intake session.

Prior to the intake interview

What can you tell your kids? We think you can certainly tell your children why you are going to participate in this programme. But since we regularly get the question, we give an example:

> We are going to participate in a programme called No Kids in the Middle, which was made for children, because children suffer from parents who often disagree, like we do. In the programme, they are going to help us to have less tension, which is nice for you and for all of us. It has all been going on for so long already and we all want more peace and quiet and to get on with our lives. Of course, we don't know for sure yet, but we hope it will help. And we are going to do it with other parents and other children. You will come in a group of children who are all in the same situation. When the group starts, the therapists who work with the children will explain everything to you about it and you can ask questions about it. And dad/mum and I come in a group with parents who all want to do things differently. I find it quite exciting, and I really want to try it.

The intake interview

After you have arrived, we start together: parents, children and all therapists together in the same room. This takes only a short while. After that, the children's therapist will take your child to another room and explain to your child what the children's group is about.

Each of you will have a short conversation with one of the parent therapists. During this conversation you can tell how the conflicts with the other parent affect you, what shocks or has shocked you so much. This can be about the divorce process, but also about the relationship before the divorce, or about other shocking experiences in your life that are connected to it. Two questions that are important for the second intake are: What do you want to achieve for the children? And what do you want to achieve yourself? You can think about these questions in advance.

GROUP THERAPY FOR HIGH-CONFLICT DIVORCE

The information evening for your social network

Between the intake interview and the start of the parent and children's groups, we organise an information evening for you and for the people around you who are important to you. This evening is not meant for the children. The evening is anonymous, like an information evening at school. Only the therapists introduce themselves. We provide information about the programme, and everyone can ask questions. Parents and the people who have come along do not get into a conversation with each other. You do not have to worry about whether you have to tell something about yourself. You do not have to answer questions, either, if you do not want to. In some cases, the mutual social networks have not seen each other for years. That is why we do not make things unnecessarily stressful. You and your network only need to listen, and you may ask questions.

Assignment

Find out who in your social network knows you well, supports you and is involved with the children. This could be your father, mother, brother, sister, friend, new (current) partner, colleague, or someone else. Also consider who is most critical about your participation in No Kids in the Middle. This person is also very welcome at the information evening.

There will also be two young people from Villa Pinedo with a coach. Villa Pinedo is an organisation of and for children of divorced parents. Just take a look at the website: www.villapinedo.nl/English/.

The evening is an important step in the project. All parents come, and we ask each parent to bring along people, at least two and at the most five. New (current) partners are very welcome. They can be very important in supporting the parent and the children, and also in continuing the therapy! The same goes for grandparents. Even though it is sometimes very painful for a parent when the other parent's new partner is there, or when his parents are there, we hope that this first step can be taken because it is important for the children.

We ask you to let the therapists know at least one week before the information evening who you will bring along.

Homework for session 1

Purpose of the homework

The homework for this session is a preparation for the first session.

Assignment 1.1

Write down for yourself what you want to achieve with this programme for the children. We will ask you to share this with the other parents.

GROUP THERAPY FOR HIGH-CONFLICT DIVORCE

Homework for session 2

Purpose of the homework

The purpose of the homework for this session is to help you better recognise the patterns in which you have ended up as parents. That you will see what reaction your behaviour evokes in the other parent and vice versa, and that, in doing so, you maintain a pattern. We have already discussed these patterns in session 1.

Destructive communication patterns

Parents who have separated and have a lot of mutual tension are caught in destructive communication patterns. These patterns are the enemy of relationships and make good intentions invisible because mistrust and suspicion become dominant. There are three basic patterns in which people can become entangled and which make the relationship increasingly unsafe and hopeless (see Figure 1):

1 The first pattern: approaching – approaching.
2 The second pattern: approaching – averting.
3 The third pattern: averting–averting.

An example

A approaches B by e-mail, phone, message or in person and wants to make something clear to B. A wants, for instance, that B pays closer attention to Tommy's gluten-free diet, as Tommy always suffers from stomach ache after having been at B's. If the relationship is good, B will listen to this, reassure A and thank A for showing concern. If, however, a high-conflict relationship has already been established, the destructive patterns become active.

Approaching–approaching

This pattern is characterised by blaming back and forth. When A calls about Tommy's stomach ache, B will strike back and say, for instance:

> You are way too much involved with Tommy with all your rules; it gives him a stomach ache. I cannot stand that either. I am glad I do not have to suffer from that anymore. When he is at my place, he never complains about a stomach ache.

The basic pattern is that A wants to make something clear to B and convince B, while B wants to make something clear to A and wants to convince A of being right. It makes no difference whether this cycle is started by A or B. And because neither A nor B feels heard, recognised or understood, the blaming will become more and more intense, and corresponding emotions will be increasingly desperate. This pattern will escalate.

Approaching–averting

When A calls B about Tommy's stomach ache, B may also hold off. B feels criticised and attacked by A and sees no sense in communicating. Communication is blocked (telephone, WhatsApp, mail, Facebook, etc.). As a result, A will feel increasingly powerless and will take even more trouble to reach B: 'After all, it is about my child.' But the more A approaches B, the more B will hold A off. This pattern, too, will escalate.

Averting–averting

This pattern arises when both A and B have given up communicating. A feeling of powerlessness prevails. When A and B are parents, children often become the messengers.

There is no point to it
Never mind . . .
Listen to me once
Can you, for once, keep the agreements?
Typical you
Stop . . .
There we go again . . .
I better say nothing

Figure 1 shows that not only the parents are caught in the destructive patterns. Children are caught, too. They are caught in the middle and have no way out. Also, other people involved often get caught in the destructive patterns.

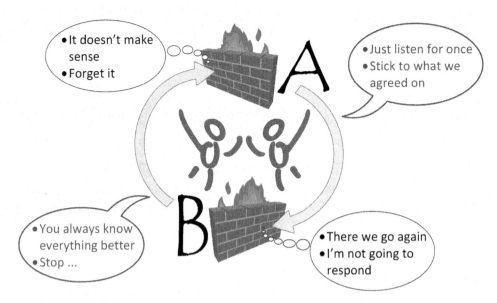

Figure 1 Destructive communication patterns

GROUP THERAPY FOR HIGH-CONFLICT DIVORCE

Questions about our destructive communication patterns

Assignment 2.1a

Tick the pattern(s) you recognise in your communication. Write your name and that of the other parent in the pattern: who does what?

☐   Approach   Avert

_____   _____

☐   Approach   Approach

_____   _____

☐   Avert   Avert

_____   _____

Assignment 2.1b

Often, people immediately recognise what the other person is doing to maintain the action–reaction pattern. This assignment is meant to let you think about what you do yourself. You may think it is a logical reaction to what the other person is doing. People who are trapped in a pattern almost always think that the other person started it and that they are only reacting to that. Try to also see your own behaviour as an 'action' to which the other person reacts, and not just as a 'reaction.'

Discuss what you have understood about it with people from your network. Try to explain what destructive communication patterns are and how they make it impossible to find solutions. If they understand it, you have been able to explain it clearly.

If you cannot work it out, read the explanation about destructive communication patterns again as explained on page XX. Ask the people in your network if they recognise one or more patterns in you and the other parent. Talk about a few examples of your destructive patterns. Remember that these patterns are maintained if everyone continues to respond to each other in the same way. You cannot usually prevent being hurt by something. But you can learn to react differently. How do you usually react? Ask the people in your network to help you if you cannot work it out yourself. We often hear that people who help you also recognise such patterns themselves, and we, too, can sometimes get caught in conflicts in this way. It is only human. Fortunately, it is possible to free yourself from that.

With this assignment, we ask you to recognise the destructive patterns. You do not have to change anything about your own reactions yet. It may make you feel powerless if you start to recognise the pattern better without knowing how you could react differently. The group and your network will help you with that.

 ## Assignment 2.1c

Now put yourself in your child(ren)'s shoes. Imagine they witness the pattern you ticked. You may think that this never happens in your case because you always keep things out of the child's sight. Try to imagine it anyway. Of the many children who participated in No Kids in the Middle, we know that they perceive much more than parents and social workers together could have suspected.

Write down what you think your child feels.

_____

_____

_____

_____

_____

GROUP THERAPY FOR HIGH-CONFLICT DIVORCE

Text blocks children

Angelina: When my parents thought I was asleep, I heard them arguing on the phone.

Colin: From the way my mother pressed the keys on the laptop I could tell if she was e-mailing with my father or with a friend.

Debbie: My father hardly ever responded to messages from my mother. 'That crap,' he used to say. My mother would make me pass on messages to him. I would often go back to my mother's house with a stomach ache if my father hadn't answered. Sometimes I came up with an excuse or I thought up an answer.

Raahim: I saw my mother's phone, open on the table, and read all of my father's words of abuse in a message to her.

Text blocks parents

Robert: While on vacation, I just turned off the phone and told the children to do the same. She kept sending e-mails and messages. I came back from vacation even more stressed out than when I left.

Lorraine: Their grandmother had been admitted to hospital . . . The children need to know things like that! And there was no way he could be reached. How on earth is that possible? I was ready to get into the car and drive up there. Eventually, I managed to reach him via the campsite owner. Well, obviously it made his highness very angry.

Helen: I've simply blocked him from everything. From Facebook, the mail, WhatsApp. Really everything. I don't care. I don't want that poison in my life anymore.

John: She is able to make me flip from calm to furious in no time. She manages to do so over and over again. It seems as if that has become her life's goal or something. And, no, when she acts like that, I'm not so friendly anymore. There was this one time, I couldn't hold back and I called her names on the phone.

Documentary about celebrity Frénk van der Linden: *Lost Connection: the Divorce of My Parents*

The parents of Frénk van der Linden divorced when he was thirteen. His mother fell in love with another man and left the family. The children stayed with their father. Frénk van der Linden no longer wanted contact with his mother. He tore up or burned the letters she sent. He did that in front of his father to show him how loyal he was.

In the meantime, Frénk's mother passed away. But at the time of the documentary, both parents were still alive and old. And they still refused to see each other. They hadn't spoken to each other for forty years. Filmmaker Gisèla Mallant followed Frénk van der Linden for the documentary *Lost Connection: the Divorce of My Parents*. In his parents' houses, Van der Linden talked about the arguments, the divorce and their lives at the time.

 ## Assignment 2.2a
Read the story of the documentary *Lost Connection* by Frénk van der Linden.

 ## Assignment 2.2b
Answer the following questions:

What destructive communication patterns do you see between Frénk's parents? Averting–averting

_____

_____

In what behaviour of the parents do you recognise this?

_____

_____

_____

What does this story show about the impact of the high-conflict divorce on Frénk's adult life?

_____

_____

_____

_____

What did it mean for Frénk and his sister?

_____

_____

_____

Assignment 2.2c

Check your network

Let the people in your network read the story too.

How did the network react?

_____

_____

_____

_____

Lost Connection

'I never want to see your mother again. I'd rather die.' Angry words spoken by my father, at the end of the documentary *Lost Connection*, which I made a few years ago about the divorce of my parents. What started as a hopeful project ended in bitterness. When I started the film together with director Gisela Mallant, I cherished the illusion that little by little I could make my mother and father understand a little more about each other by interviewing them both at length about the loss of their love. But no.

For forty years, Jan van der Linden and Erica van den Brink did not exchange a word. My mother's leaving, because of a passionate relationship with another man, aroused hatred in my father that lasted for decades. My sister Desirée and I, adolescents, were every bit as bad: we wrote a letter to the judge who handled the case and let him know that we did not want to have contact with 'that bitch' anymore. And if he would award custody of us to dad immediately. That's exactly what happened. For twelve years we tore up letters from the woman who had given birth to us, for twelve years we hang up when she called, for twelve years we walked past her when she was waiting for us at the school fence.

No one smells like your mother. The moment I held her in my arms again at the age of 25, I smelled: this is the woman who gave birth to me. Desirée and I rebuilt the connection with her (meanwhile staying close with our father), and that harmony lasted until she disappeared into the mists of Alzheimer's disease.

The moment the diagnosis of dementia was made, I realised that not much more than a year was left for us to make an attempt, in some clarity, to put an end to our shared family pain. Because whichever way you look at it: father, mother, daughter, son, all of us suffered from the situation, from the silence and the hiding, from this cold war. Hence the plan to make a TV film in which my father and mother would be interviewed separately. Both of them fully cooperated, convinced that their own story would eventually convince the other one that he/she was wrong.

After a few months of filming, my father appeared to stick to his guns: no, he didn't want to speak to my mother (who really wanted to talk and longed for forgiveness) (Visser & van Lawick, 2021) under no condition. I hadn't experienced a bigger disappointment than that in my life before. As a journalist, but also as a son, I had come to the conclusion that there are no black-and-white conflicts. Not between parties, not between chip shop owners, not between countries, not between lovers. Every step taken by one person also shapes the step taken by the other one and vice versa. There is always shared guilt. A week before the broadcast of *Lost Connection* I called my father. Dad, are you 100% sure that you never want to see mum again?

He sighed. And again he sighed.
'Dad?'
'Well, all right then, boy.'

A few days later he threw his arms around my mother at his home in Lelystad. 'I've never been so sad as when you left me,' he said. 'And maybe I've never been as happy as I am now.' For three hours they were talking hand in hand. How lucky they had been together those years. How wonderful their two children were. And how unfortunate that one little problem had been: those forty years of distance between them. It's a good thing that it has now been polished away.

Between the time my mother had left our house and the moment they made peace again, there had been countless years in which I had not been able to cry. As well as I could reach the emotions of others as an interviewer, as badly I could reach my own. But that evening in Lelystad, tears were pouring down my cheeks. Of happiness. And as much as the death of my mother hurt some time later: the fact that my father was standing by her coffin with a red rose made up for a lot.

People, talk. Talk to each other. Ask questions, listen, say what you have to say yourself, and free yourself from the anger with which you destroy yourself rather than the other one. The authors of this book have understood that. It took me far too much time to understand, adding unnecessary pain to the conflicts in my family. I wish others more wisdom.

Frénk van der Linden

Frénk van der Linden © Ben Kleyn

GROUP THERAPY FOR
HIGH-CONFLICT DIVORCE

Homework for session 3

 ### Purpose of the homework

In session 2 you have experienced what happens to children when parents always have conflicts. After reading the text that follows, we ask you to write something about this.

What does it do to the children?

What does it do to children when parents often disagree, have a lot of mutual tension and regularly speak ill of each other?

Children are born out of two parents and are existentially connected to them. Children are torn when these two have many conflicts, openly or covertly. Children need safety around them in order to be able to develop. They want to be able to rely on parents who have attention for their children and do everything possible to make life run smoothly for them.

If parents divorce and pay a lot of attention to their children so that they can withstand all the changes, children do not have to suffer from the divorce. Of course, children do not like all these changes, and it makes them sad to miss one of the parents on certain days. The change of house, school and neighbourhood, but also the contact with friends, with grandparents and other relatives, having to get used to new stepparents, stepbrothers and stepsisters and a new family – all this requires adjustments, and that may temporarily unbalance children.

If parents see their children through these changes in such a way that the children feel that they matter and that both parents take good care of them, they will find a new balance after a while. But when parents fight each other, this is not possible. Then a child remains off balance. The fiercer the conflicts, the more the child gets off balance. Especially when parents accuse each other and call the other a bad parent, a demon who ruins everything for them, it is very difficult for children to cope with a divorce. The child then has to live in two 'truths', two different stories, two explanations of the truth – about what 'the truth' is – and it gets confusing. And when that child wants to say something about the pain and confusion, there is a good chance that it will be used in the conflict between their parents: 'You see now what you're doing to our child!' Sometimes this is expressed to the child itself: 'Ah, that father/mother of yours!' Most parents know that they should not burden their children with this and hope that their child will not notice the tensions. However, children do notice. Mira:

> It's in the air, everywhere, I can see it in mum's or dad's face, I notice it when they send angry messages to each other on WhatsApp, I also hear how dad talks to Ellen about mum, and how mum talks to grandma about dad, even though they think I don't hear it.

Children can react very differently to this situation. Some children completely adjust themselves so that they will not give rise to more fighting. By trying to help the parents in this way, they become a party in the conflict. Apparently, nothing is wrong, but when these children start to express themselves, they appear to suffer a lot from the conflict between the parents. Other children are rebellious and sad and express this in many places, at home and at school. Some children suffer from loss of concentration and perform below their ability in school. Other children develop a variety of symptoms, from bedwetting, anxiety complaints, gloominess and very busy behaviour, to failure symptoms.

There is also a group that cannot keep on living in two truths. Almost all people in the parents' networks side with one of the parents, and sometimes children do the same. These children decide to live in 'one truth'; they side with one parent and do not want to see the other parent. However painful that may be, it is understandable. Siblings sometimes divide this up – one 'sides with' the mother, and the other 'sides with' the father. What makes it even sadder is that, by doing so, they often lose contact with each other as well – in practice, because they don't or barely see each other anymore, but also psychologically, because it is difficult to keep in touch with someone who lives in another truth.

When parents no longer fight, are friendly with each other more or less frequently and are also able to let go of each other, then the children will do better too. Often the symptoms will disappear, and children will do better at school and start developing again.

Reflection

Assignment 3.1a

What did it do to you?

In session 2, you sat on a children's chair while the other parents acted out the destructive communication patterns. All parents usually manage to put themselves in the children's shoes. Parents in the children's chairs often feel strong emotions. Sometimes parents feel little or nothing at all. These are all reactions to a high level of stress: your body reacts by wanting to attack (getting angry), by fleeing (feeling small, wanting to leave, wanting to disappear), or by freezing (being numb with fear or feeling very sad). Write down what happened to you in the children's chair.

I felt:

_____

_____

I thought:

_____

_____

In my body I felt (also write down where you felt it):

_____

_____

I hoped or wished:

_____

_____

And this is what I think and feel now that I have written it all down:

_____

_____

_____

Assignment 3.1b

Check your network

> The people in your network are there to support you, and they would like to do so too. Probably, they often don't really know what they can do. Sometimes people from your network support you by talking to you about how bad the other parent is and how wrong he or she does everything. Although that may feel good for a while, it does not help.
>
> ## An example
>
> A grandmother called out to her daughter, 'The things he does to you, I just hate that guy.'
>
> The daughter, who took part in the parent group, suddenly realised what was happening: it felt good, but it did not really help. She said: 'Mum, it is nice of you to support me, but it is not the way to help me, he is still the father of my children, and I will have to get along with him anyway.' She was amazed herself at the effect this had on her and on her mother.
>
> Two weeks later, they both attended the final musical of their daughter Michelle and grandma and dad could greet each other, albeit coolly. It was clear to everyone how relieved and happily Michelle reacted.
>
> People from the network around the parents may unintentionally reinforce destructive patterns, especially by also speaking ill of the other parent. They can also help to reconcile, on the one hand, by acknowledging that things are very painful and difficult and, on the other, by highlighting a good quality or memory. This is difficult, but it can free everyone from crushing negative spirals.
>
> Talking to people around you about what the conflict between parents does to children can be an important step in understanding what it is all about in the parent group.

Explain to one or more people in your network what it means for children if parents continue to fight by blaming each other or, on the contrary, by not communicating, by withdrawing and fighting in silence. Also explain the exercise with the children's chairs and tell them what it was like for you.

Literally write down the reactions of people from your network:

1. _____
2. _____
3. _____
4. _____

What remarks are helpful? How?

___

Assignment 3.1c

What does your child notice about the destructive patterns?

Now, answer the question 'What does the conflict between their parents mean for the children?' with your own child in mind. It helps to take a recent situation as an example. Discuss the following with your network:

- How does your child show that something is bothering him or her?
- How does your child notice that you as parents disagree and argue about that?

When I look at my child, I see, notice or feel:

My child feels

___

My child thinks

___

My child does

___

What my network noticed in _____ (name of the child):

___

Recognising and changing destructive patterns

By now, you surely recognise the destructive patterns that are active between you and the other parent. Maybe you will read the article about the destructive patterns again some time. Pay special attention to what you do yourself, what position you take in the vicious problem cycle and how you approach the other.

Assignment 3.2a

What goes differently?

We are curious to hear a concrete example of a situation in which you have been able to change something, where you have done something differently as a result of which the communication went differently. It can be a small example. Things threatened to repeat themselves, but because you did something differently, things went differently.

Can you describe that here?

_____

_____

_____

Which pattern threatened to emerge?

- Approaching–averting
- Approaching–approaching
- Averting–averting

In Figure 2, describe what happened when the pattern became active, what you did differently and how things went differently then. You can also describe what the other person did differently. And then write down what you noticed in the children.

What I did:

_____

_____

_____

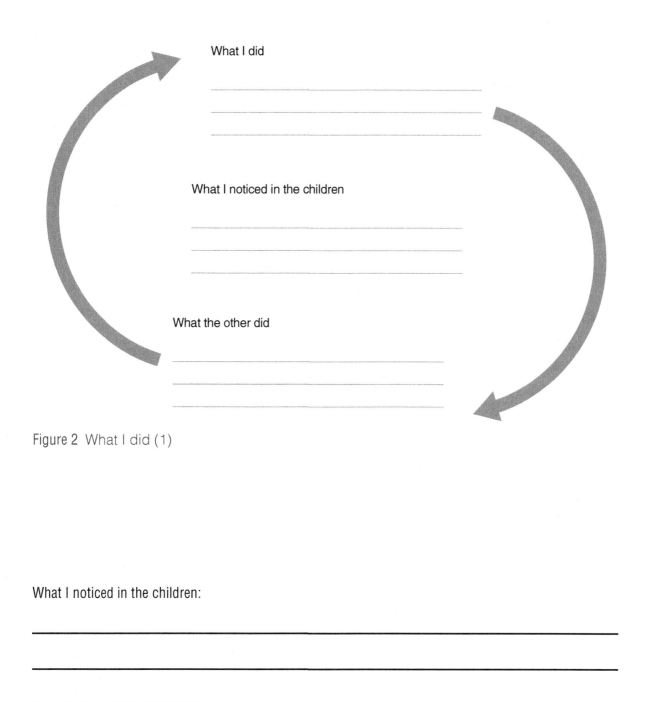

Figure 2 What I did (1)

What I noticed in the children:

_____

_____

_____

What the other did:

_____

_____

_____

If you have not managed to do something differently yet, you can think about how you would like to do things differently.

Assignment 3.2b

In order not to keep getting caught in the same hopeless spirals, I intend to (continue to) do the following things differently:

_____

_____

_____

Assignment 3.2c

Make it your goal to put in practice what you wrote down under assignment 3.2 in the coming weeks. Remember that you do this because you want to get the children out of the middle, and how much you also want to free yourself, so that you can spend your energy on positive things. And help yourself by realising that this is not an exercise that can make the other parent behave differently. This is an exercise that helps to get children out of the middle. Even if the other parent continues to react in the same way, you have changed the destructive pattern for your children by reacting differently yourself. You free yourself, as it were. You no longer let your reaction depend on how the other parent reacts, but you decide for yourself how you react for the sake of your child's well-being.

In the group we ask you if and how this worked out and what effect you see in the children.

Assignment 3.2d

Don't forget to involve your network. Ask for help. Ask them to think along and for tips so that you no longer get caught in these destructive patterns. Then the children can start to feel relief and space.

Tips I got from my network:

_____

_____

_____

Assignment 3.2e
Small changes

From now on, keep a log of things that have already changed a little, of things that you do differently yourself. And what goes differently. Try to discover what makes the children happy.

_____

_____

_____

It takes two people to maintain the negative cycle

Gym clothes

A father who is very upset, since it is the umpteenth time that the mother has not given the gym clothes to his eight-year-old son for school, comes up with the following idea. He decides not to complain about it to the mother anymore and not to talk about it to his child anymore. However, he agrees with the schoolteacher that he will leave a bag with extra gym clothes in school just in case.

A mother of a thirteen-year-old daughter also decides not to fight about it with the father anymore, but to tackle her daughter about it instead. After all, she is big enough now to think of her gym clothes herself. So far, her daughter has had to stay behind three times. 'Hope that she learns from it' is the reaction of the mother.

Unwanted messages

The many messages and long e-mails from a mother drives a father completely crazy. He notices that it causes a lot of tension between them as parents when he ignores the messages. And their child feels that tension. Together with people from his network, he comes up with the following idea: a sister is willing to help by screening the long messages and getting the essence out of them. Then he writes a short reaction. Sister checks the message to make sure that it does not contain escalating content. Then he sends the message. This is killing two birds with one stone: de-escalation, and the child is no longer the messenger who has to pass on messages because the father ignored the e-mails.

The story

In session 1 we explained the destructive communication patterns. Session 2 was about the impact of your conflict between the two of you on your child. In session 3 we discussed the story for your child about why you do not live under one roof (anymore).

Michael: I was eight when my parents broke up. The only thing I heard in the beginning was: 'Mum and dad are always arguing and we don't love each other anymore like we used to.'

But I just felt that there was more to it than that. Mum was angry a lot, also with us, and said very ugly things about dad. And dad never wanted to drop us off at the door, so we always had to walk the last part to mum with our bags.

He never wanted to know how it had been at mum's. Mum always wanted to know how things had gone at dad's, but after a while I didn't dare say anything about that because she was always critical and I started to feel like a traitor.

Now I am fourteen and I still don't know a thing. Mum says that dad only thought of himself and always left her alone with us. Dad says that mum had fallen in love with someone else. I don't understand a thing anymore. They each tell something different and I am not much wiser for it. Maybe someday I'll find out.

Emma: What I really hated was when they said: 'When you're older, we will tell you the whole story.' Right now I am sixteen and I still don't know very much, except that what they say doesn't make any sense.

Jordan: My parents each tell something different. And the terrible thing is that my grandmother tells exactly the same story as my mother and my grandmother from my father's side tells exactly the same as my father. But somehow something is not right. Who am I supposed to believe? I don't think they understand how that works for a child, that it completely confuses me.

Flora: Mum says that dad can't take care of us because he is away so often away and that his new girlfriend is no better than him. Dad says that mum's story is not true and that that is the very problem. That mum is always interrogating us, that she wants to interfere with everything and, in doing so, is damaging us.

> **Andreas**: I miss my father and I miss my mother. It's so weird. All of my friends' parents either live together or are divorced. But my parents never lived together. Why not? And why are they arguing? Dad says: 'Ask your mother.' And my mother says: 'Ask your father.' At school, the children often ask me if my parents are divorced. But they are not. Now, what am I supposed to say?

It is important that children have a coherent life story.

The importance of a coherent life story

A coherent life story ensures mental well-being and healthy identity development. The story of the divorce of the parents is an important part of that life story. But in their conflicts, parents often tell their own version of why they no longer live together. They often point to each other as the culprit. As a result, the children lack a coherent story. These contradictory 'truths' easily confuse them. Mother says: 'Dad doesn't want to see you, he's too busy with other things.' Father says: 'Why don't you come more often, I see so little of you. I bet your mum doesn't want you to see me.' And the child gets totally confused. Do parents lie?

Write a letter to your child

You all have an explanation for why it all went so wrong. And in that explanation the other parent most likely receives the blame. You yourself are rather the victim of the misbehaviour by the other. That has become a story that you have told many times to many people. Both stories, however, are very confusing for the children and for other people around you, because they do not fit together. That is why we ask you to write a story about the divorce in which the other person does not receive all the blame, in which the other person remains whole. You do this in a form that we will describe here.

Write a letter to your child* in which you explain why you do not or no longer live together. If your child is still very young, imagine that he/she is already a little older – for example, twelve years old.

You write the letter alone, not together.

Describe, briefly, why you do not or no longer live together as parents. Explain in simple language how this came about. Do this in a way that will not confuse your child or make it feel uncomfortable when listening to it. Do this in such a way that your child will not feel guilty because it may start to think that it is the reason why you broke up.

Important in writing this letter to your child is that the parents accept each other as they are. It is okay when the letter shows that the two of you are different. And also that there are different reasons why you do not (no longer) live together or have never lived together.

What you should not do in your letter is blame the other person of everything, put the other in a bad light, make all kinds of accusations, embarrass the other or reject him or her as the parent of the child.

Try to write the letter in such a way that the other parent can listen to the story. Try to formulate your sentences in such a way that they reflect your good intentions. After all, you are setting an example for your child. Through this letter, you show that you can and want to accept the other person as he or she is, how difficult and painful the situation may be and despite your disagreements. Show that you acknowledge the other person as the parent of your child, even though you no longer live under one roof. You may have different opinions. Children can handle that well as long as these differences do not lead to demonisation.

So write the story with respect – respect for yourself, for your child and for the other as a parent. Only then will it become a story that your child can tell when he or she wants to answer the question: Why are your parents divorced? Why don't your parents live together anymore? For that is a question that will be asked many more times in his or her life. It is a question that bothers many children, even if it is not asked. Many children struggle with it. It affects the way they think about relationships and it can make them confused and insecure when they enter into a relationship themselves.

So write a story that your child can live and grow up with, without getting confused about relationships, without feeling embarrassed or guilty. Because deep down, your child loves two parents, both of you.

Read the story to people in your network and then consider again if this would be a story that the other parent can hear, that your child can live with and will bring peace and quiet to their lives. A story that acknowledges the differences but takes away the tension that only causes confusion inside.

In session 3 you will have the opportunity to read your letter in a small group of three parent couples. Make sure that the reading does not take longer than five to seven minutes. If the letter is longer, make it shorter with the help and cooperation of people from your network so that only the truly essential sentences are left. You will all get a chance to read your letter. You are not supposed to already read or give the letter to your child(ren). That is not important at this stage and can always be done later. The letter will need time to 'mature.'

Take the letter to the third session!

Everyone will read the letter in session 3. We make two groups of three parent couples. So you sit together and listen to each other's letter.

Dear Sophie,

When mum and I met, we were young. I was still studying and mum already worked as a primary school teacher. Thanks to her job, I was able to finish my studies, for which I am grateful to her. We had a good time together and did nice things. We loved the same music, camping and doing things with friends. When we had just moved to a place together, mum turned out to be pregnant, you were coming. That was a surprise, but a very nice one, because we were immediately crazy about you. You were an easy baby. Mum worked and I was at home with you, because I was still studying. Mum was obviously jealous that I could spend so much time with you and she could not because she had to work. When I had to work hard for an exam, grandma came to babysit. Grandma knows you very well and you often go to her. When I graduated, I immediately got a job at Randstad Uitzendbureau, and I still work there today. Mum started to work less in order to be able to spend more time with you. And then the arguing started. I wanted to spend a lot of time with you when I was at home, but mum thought I was too rough with you, or that I kept you awake for too long. And I thought that mum was too much of a 'head-parent', as if I were employed by her. I am sure you've been bothered by our arguments. I realise that and I am sorry. You are not to blame for the fights. We did it together and we did it badly. In the end, we were only fighting. It didn't work anymore. Then I left. I first went to live in the flat and now I live in the new house. And there I met Anna, with whom I live now. Mum and I kept arguing after the divorce, which is very bad for you. I really hope that we can stop that. I will do everything I can to achieve that. Because I love you and I will always love you.

Big kiss, your dad

Check your network

Read the letter to people in your network. Check once again if this is a story that the other parent can listen to and that your child(ren) can live with and can bring peace and quiet. If it takes more than five minutes to read the letter, make it shorter, with or without the help of people from your network. Children prefer short and clear stories. Take the letter, written or printed out, to session 3.

You are not supposed to already read or give the letter to your child(ren). That can always be done later. The letter will need time to 'mature.'

The tragedy of life

Many issues are never resolved because the differences between the parents are too great. Research shows that 69 percent of issues between people, even if they have an extremely good relationship, are unsolvable. So you will keep thinking differently about these issues. These unsolvable issues can cause a lot of tension, dissatisfaction, pain and sadness, however.

> Why can't he just see that it cannot go on like this?
> Why can't she just understand that I can't agree to this?

The prospect that certain painful issues will never be resolved is part of the tragedy of everyone's life. Everyone has to live with the fact that they've never had perfect parents, their parents will have their good sides and their bad sides, but most parents are good enough. Children need to learn to live with the parents they have, and parents need to learn to live with the children they have, children need to learn to live with the sisters and brothers they have, exes need to learn to live with their ex, and stepparents need to learn to live with the stepchildren and vice versa. We can go on like this. People who can live with the situation as it is and can accept that there is much that cannot be changed have a better life.

> 'My children are the only thing I have left. If I were to give in to that woman again, I'll lose them too! I won't let that happen, I won't give in. I will never bow to her ideas, I stick to my point of view.'
>
> 'The cooperation with my ex is in a deadlock, he is so extreme in his opinions, there is no way to get through that. He wants to destroy me!'

Daring to face the tragedy means that you resign yourself to not being able to influence everything. That you have no control over the other person. That the other person may possibly never change and that you will continue to be confronted with this every now and then. That that is a tragedy that won't change. That you can only change how you deal with it, in a way that makes it easier for your children. This is perhaps the most difficult thing and, at the same time, the most liberating in the whole project. It also allows the children to deal with the tragedy of life. After all, they have the parents they have, with their beautiful and vulnerable sides.

This way of looking at things helps to put things into perspective. It promotes thinking in colours instead of in black and white. This way of looking at things helps to accept the pain and sorrow by realising that life has turned out differently than you had hoped for. And that helps you to make compromises that allow for more peace for everyone, even if it does not seem to be the ideal solution.

> It feels like my children are the only ones I have left. I really never expected life to turn out as it has. When I signed up for this programme, I often wondered: how on earth did we end up here. It is how it is. Our relationship has had a lot to endure and that is painful for both of us. And for the children, too.
>
> The cooperation with my ex is really stuck. I can't change him. That's an illusion, I understand now. It's a pity that life has taken this course. We both had different expectations and they didn't come true. It does not help to blame someone for that. Not the least the children. I'd better look at what is going well.

Tips for all divorced parents from our ambassador Mark Tuitert:

That my parents broke up came as a surprise to me. It was not an option that I had thought of as a child. There had been fights, but fights happen everywhere, right? I was eighteen when my parents got divorced. I was about to break through as a professional skater and went to live with my mother together with two younger brothers. For a child it is difficult, they are torn by a feeling of loyalty and love for both parents. At home, the situation was often quite explosive. After the divorce, I had hardly any contact with my father for five years.

What I found most disturbing was that my parents reacted to each other as small children, with all the common tactics. Unreasonableness, anger, exaggeration, I've seen it all. It made me angry. Sometimes there was a wall between my parents and there was nobody to break it.

Therefore, I would like to give parents a few tips:

Don't react in the moment. You are adults. Let it show. The pain you have as a parent does not go away and is inside you. And no matter how hard that may be, keep your children out of it.

Never ask your child to make a choice! Don't judge the other in front of your children, never! Children will form their own picture. Give them the space to do so in their own way.

Agree on rules on how to argue. Don't do it when the children are around and when they are, agree to make up in front of them. It will shape their picture of the future.

Listen to your child's feelings, but don't make it emotionally charged. Explain what decisions you make and why, but don't bother your children with your emotional life. Put aside your own feelings (temporarily). That is something to share with friends and relatives.

Luckily, contact with my father, which I cut off at first, has been restored. Things are going better now than ever and I am now a father myself of Anna (5) and Tom (3). The divorce of my parents has cost me a lot of energy, but has also taught me valuable lessons. I have seen how difficult it is to keep emotions at bay, almost impossible. But that's exactly why it's so crucial . . .

Regards, Mark Tuitert.

Mark Tuitert, Mel Butter

GROUP THERAPY FOR HIGH-CONFLICT DIVORCE

Homework for session 4

 ## Purpose of the homework

Keep working on your letter. If required, change your letter based on the feedback you have received on your letter. The homework is also a preparation for session 4. In this session you will have to bring symbols for the positive qualities of the other parent *as a parent*, and we will work on issues involving the children which you have trouble resolving.

Symbols

We have been talking about demonisation and destructive patterns. It turns out that changes usually come about sooner and faster if you focus on making positive moves.

Research has shown that it is very important for children to be able to recognise and express positive things about the parenting of the other person. In this way, children learn that their parents can make mistakes, but that they also have positive, powerful sides. Our research also showed how important it is that parents can forgive themselves and others, that they can see themselves and others as people with good and bad sides, and that the people around them also take that step. Forgiving (Visser & van Lawick, 2021) can be pretty difficult. It should be possible to think of something that you value in the other person as a parent. And if that does not work, look at it through the eyes of your child: what does he or she see?

 ## Assignment 4.1a

Look for a maximum of two items that show how you can say something positive about the other person in his or her role as a parent.

For example: 'I brought this round stone because to me it symbolises the way he, as a father, is always ready to take them to their sports clubs, come rain or shine. He is indestructible when it comes to that. It makes me happy for the children.'

It can also be an item that tells a story. For example: 'I found this item at home, it is a . . . She once gave it to our daughter when she went away for a weekend, in case she would get homesick. And that is what I found so sweet and caring of her, as a mother. She is still like that.'

The item can also be a symbol for something connected to everyday life: a ball for 'playing together', a spoon for 'great cooking' so that the children eat healthy food, a book for 'reading to the children', anything is possible as long as it is connected to parenting.

Would you like more information? Then read the comprehensive text on symbols.

Assignment 4.1b

I have found these symbols:

_____

_____

_____

These symbols express why the children are lucky to have the other as a parent, because:

_____

_____

_____

Assignment 4.1c

Bring the items you have chosen to the fourth session!

About symbols

Parents who participated in the programme before indicated that they found this an important but sometimes also a difficult assignment. With this assignment you give the other person a compliment about his or her parenting. That is not easy if you have felt for years that the other person is making things only difficult or is doing things the wrong way. For children, it is very important that you can still see the other person as a parent who is good enough. They need it. You do this assignment for them.

Remember that this assignment is not about your relationship as partners but about parenting. Ask yourself this question: which quality of the other parent can make the children happy?'

Children need to learn that no one is perfect or all bad. Especially when it comes to their own parents (see also appendix 1).

> **Rickie (11 years old)**: I don't think she was aware that I heard it, but I was so happy to hear mum say to grandma that dad always takes me to soccer practice and makes sure that I get there on time.

> **Ebony (8 years old)**: Dad told me that he believed that mum really took good care of us, that he really didn't worry about that. I was so happy to hear that he said something nice.

> **Leroy (13 years old)**: I never feel like going to dad's house. I don't like having to go there because he is always busy and we hardly do anything together. Usually, my sister and I are alone with his new girlfriend. Mum knows that but she never says anything nasty about it. I appreciate that about her. She often says: 'If you don't like it, then talk about it with him. He is just a busy man, but he'll really listen to you. He can do that.'

Preferably, choose a symbol related to something recent, something that you now appreciate of the other as a parent.

You can also include a smile.

> I brought this laughing machine because Jasper always makes funny jokes and makes the kids laugh.

You may also bring items that symbolise a nice memory that the child may have of being with the other parent.

> I took this postcard because she always did a lot of things with the children when on holiday. The children inherited her creativity.

It can also be an item that tells a story.

> I found this at home, it is a soft toy. She once gave it to our daughter when she went away for a weekend, in case she got homesick. And I found that so sweet and caring of her as a mother.

The items can be anything, as long as they can serve as a symbol. Some parents start by looking for a symbol and then think of what they will say about the other parent.

Assignment 4.2a

Feedback on the letter

You have read your letter in the group. The other parents, in the children's chairs, gave feedback by moving closer or away or by not moving. Did 'the children' come closer? Can you write down in the left column why that was? Did they move away from certain words or sentences? Can you write something about that in the right column? Did they perhaps stay where they were? What was the message behind that?

Came closer
Did not move
Moved away

Assignment 4.2b

Read again

Read your letter again, preferably with someone from your network, and consider if you want to change it or if you like it as it is.

In preparation for the fourth session

Assignment 4.3a

Issues

Together with the people from your network, think of an issue you would like to raise in one of the upcoming sessions. It has to be about something that bothers you and that preoccupies your mind. Something you think is important for the parenting of your children. Choose a small, not too big issue. Parenting arrangements as a subject for an issue is far too complex. Choose, for instance, an issue about clothing, different rules or the arrangements for a particular holiday.

Please note down below a maximum of three issues you would like to raise. Then ask all the people in your network to think about whether these issues are too big or not.

1. _____

2. _____

3. _____

In the group session we will discuss these issues. We have a way to do this that we will explain during the session. The goal of discussing issues during the session is to find a way that allows you to stay calm and to keep listening, even if you don't agree with each other at all. Discuss with your network how you can discuss an issue in such a way that you really make progress. Not that a solution has to be found, because that only rarely happens. It is nice when there is some movement, and who knows, maybe you will work it out.

> **Father**: If I understand you correctly, you would like the children to be with you on Mother's Day, and you find it difficult that it is exactly in the weekend that they are supposed to be with me.

> **Mother**: I do understand that you want to see Tom a bit longer in the weekend. He is such a nice kid.

A father tells that his son keeps telling him that he wants to be with him more often and longer, but his mother tells him that when their son is with her, he says he doesn't want to go to his father. In the past he would have fought over this, but now he wants to try to approach it differently. He brings it up as an issue in the group sessions. Together with his buddy, he comes to the conclusion that, as parents, they will not be able to work it out now. He decides to share this very conclusion with his son, without putting his mother in a bad light. And he advises his son to talk to his mother about it and to let her know his wishes.

The parents participating in No Kids in the Middle discuss very different issues: about the holidays, about clothes that are returned unwashed, about grandma's birthday or about the children's diet. When discussing the issues, always keep the children in mind. Discussing these issues is an exercise in talking about difficult and often emotionally charged issues while keeping the children in mind. This is because the children feel the tension surrounding these issues, even though they may not witness the confrontations about them.

The aim is to see where you can change your approach of the conversation. The following themes, which you have already practiced, will again play a part:

- keeping the children in mind (how does it affect the children?);
- making sure that destructive patterns do not become active.

Assignment 4.3b

Taking steps

Discuss with people around you what you can do to stay out of the destructive pattern. Mail an assignment you have given yourself to the therapists of the parent group at least one week before the next session. What do you want to practice to improve the situation for the children? This can be anything, as long as it is something that you can influence yourself.

For example:

Do: I am going to try to stay kind when I have contact with the other person. This is possible because you can influence it yourself.

Don't: I am going to wait until the other person treats me with respect. This is not possible, because you are not able to influence that.

GROUP THERAPY FOR HIGH-CONFLICT DIVORCE

Comprehensive chapter

Escalation and de-escalation

This chapter was added to pay extra attention to the question: how come tensions keep rising, and why is it so difficult to break them? In this chapter we will discuss the stress system. It will make you better understand why you can get so angry or anxious in certain situations or by certain reactions, or why, on the contrary, you may freeze and no longer feel anything.

We have made assignments to go with the theory. By following the steps in these assignments, you will learn how your stress system works and what vulnerabilities and triggers are important to you. You will learn how to calm down yourself. It will help you to break the vicious destructive patterns. These are assignments that you can do in the coming weeks, but which can also help you avoid falling back into the destructive pattern.

Escalating conflicts

After the first few sessions, many parents start to wonder what they can do to improve their situation, how they can free themselves – free all of them. In order to make steps in that direction, we first discuss the subject of escalations: why do certain conflicts keep escalating?

An example: Lilian and Lewis

The agreement is that Lilian takes her children Jason (10 years old) and Laura (8 years old) to their father Lewis on Saturday at ten o'clock. Lewis is planning to go to the tropical swimming paradise with the children and has agreed to meet a friend and his children there.

Lilian first has to pick up Jason at a friend's house where he stayed the night. When she gets there, it turns out that Jason and his friend Tom are still walking around in their pyjamas, and they are absorbed in their game. Mya, Tom's mother, invites Lilian in for a cup of coffee and asks the boys to get dressed. It's a cosy atmosphere, Laura is also playing and they forget the time. Suddenly Lilian jumps up, it is already half past ten. She urges Jason to get dressed quickly: 'We are going to dad's, hurry up, we are late.' Her tension spreads to the children. Mya is surprised: 'Relax, it's Saturday. Surely Lewis isn't a dictator. The children are having a good time, that is more important, isn't it?'

At eleven o'clock Lilian drives off, stressed out and thinking about what Mya had said. 'Surely he can relax a little bit. No need to behave like a dictator. He ruins everything.' In the meantime, Lewis has become annoyed about them not being there at ten o'clock. At half past ten he is angry and at eleven o'clock he is furious. She does that to annoy me, he thinks. She doesn't want me to have a nice day with the children. She has to ruin everything again.

When Lilian arrives with the children at a quarter past eleven, he is fuming. He has called his friend to tell him that he will not come to the tropical paradise and he goes on at Lilian. The children witness it and they cower. When Laura starts to cry, Lewis takes Laura and Jason inside and Lilian drives off. Laura starts crying even louder and says: 'I haven't said goodbye to mummy yet.' Jason comforts her.

Look at Figure 3. This is an example of what can happen.

As in Figure 3, a diagram can be made for both parents. Often parents trigger each other. For the children it is also possible to fill in what happens, what they experience, what they think, what they feel, what they do and what the consequences are. All these patterns become intertwined and reinforce each other.

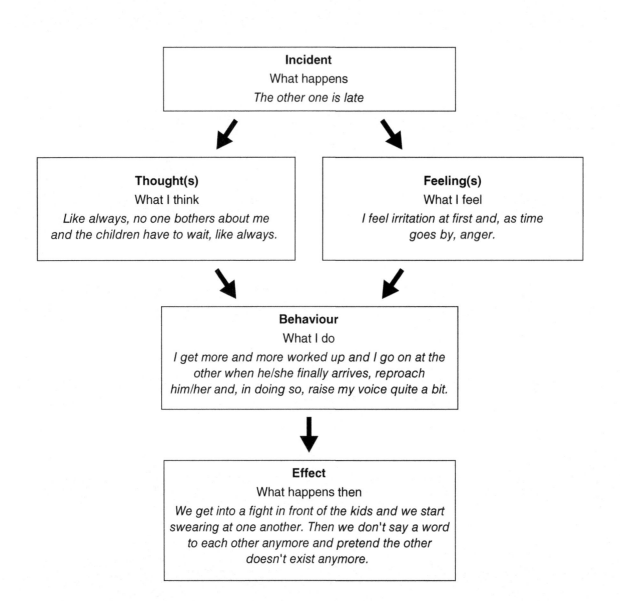

Comprehensive assignment 1

Fill in Figure 4 for yourself. This will help you to understand how conflicts escalate. In doing so, keep an example in mind.

Incident
What happens

_____

Thought(s)
What I think

_____

Feeling(s)
What I feel

_____

Behaviour
What I do

_____

Effect
What happens then

_____

Figure 4 Incident–effect

Escalating conflicts, window of tolerance, trauma and de-escalation

Lilian and Lewis got into a big fight when Lilian arrived at Lewis's place much later than agreed. Lilian was afraid of Lewis's anger, but she was also angry. ('Why does he always have to ruin everything with his anger? It had just been so nice together.') Lewis had the feeling that Lilian was pestering him and didn't want him to have a good time with the children, that she had deliberately arrived late. As a result, he felt he wasn't taken seriously, as if he didn't matter.

For Lilian, the trigger is that the other gets angry, and for Lewis, that he doesn't feel taken seriously. Often, these triggers are connected to earlier experiences – experiences in the relationship, in previous relationships or in childhood. For example, Lilian may have had an older brother who was often angry and who ruined the atmosphere at home. And in her relationship with Lewis, she has always had a lot of trouble with his angry moods. These experiences accumulate and make her more sensitive. Lewis has often felt misunderstood in his life, both by his parents and by his employer. And in the relationship with Lilian, he felt that he always had to adapt to her, that he didn't really matter. This has also increased his sensitivity.

Because of these sensitivities, Lilian and Lewis easily trigger each other and conflicts escalate quickly.

When there is increasing frustration and anger, people first get angry, then furious and finally lose their heads. In the fear variant, after being alert and vigilant, people become frightened, then panic and eventually lose their heads. Fear and anger often intertwine.

When people do not calm down in time and the escalation continues, their bodies become alarmed. Blood pressure, heart rate, muscle tension and stress hormone levels increase, and the breathing is high and accelerates. The part of the brain that is connected with 'survival' becomes active. With this reaction, the body makes sure that people can stand up for themselves. The body is ready to fight, to flee or to freeze. To be able to survive a threat, it is, you could say, a 'wise and helpful brain', because in case of a robbery it is very helpful to be able to assess whether you can attack the robber with an iron bar, whether you can still flee through an open door, or whether to act dead in order to ward off the danger. But when it comes to relational issues, these reactions are not helpful; rather, they are obstructive. Fighting, fleeing and freezing reinforce the destructive patterns, affecting the safety of the children, the parents and their network.

The speed and intensity with which people's feelings and behaviour escalate is related to their window of tolerance: the 'framework' within which people can regulate their emotions and in which they can stay connected, listen and come up with solutions. When trauma or other emotional pain affects the

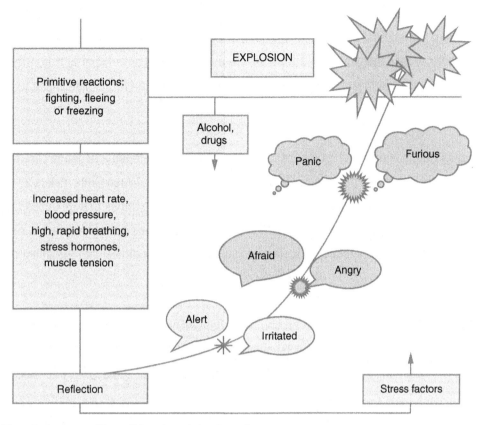

Figure 5 Escalating conflicts (Van Lawick, 2014)

tolerance for regulating emotions, when the window of tolerance is small, people are more likely to end up fighting, fleeing or freezing.

Lilian's window of tolerance for anger is not large. When someone else gets angry, her stress level quickly increases. Often she freezes and sometimes she leaves quickly or cuts herself off (fleeing). Lewis is not very tolerant when he has the feeling that nobody is considerate of him, when he has the feeling that he does not matter. Then he quickly gets very angry. Lewis's anger triggers Lilian, and Lilian's triggers Lewis.

This goes for many parents who are involved in a conflict divorce. They have often had painful and shocking experiences in the relationship with the other parent. Sometimes traumatic experiences from previous relationships or from childhood also play a role.

It is a known fact that people with shocking and sometimes traumatic experiences are more likely to react violently when they feel a threat. They have a sensitive alarm system and are quickly triggered. They get angry or scared easily or are easily blocked. The resulting behaviour can trigger a violent reaction in another person (with or without an alarm system that is just as sensitive).

If people grew up with a lot of unpleasant experiences, or if the partner relationship has been destructive for a long time and sometimes been violent, certain self-thoughts may come up that very quickly lead to intense emotions. These 'negative core thoughts' are usually untrue or only partly true. Often people know this, rationally, and yet these thoughts will be triggered quickly and immediately lead to intense emotions.

Frank grew up without having contact with his own father. He has developed a negative core thought: fathers are not important to children, I am a father, I am not important. When Odile makes a remark about his relationship with the children, he immediately thinks that she thinks that he doesn't matter as a father, and then he gets stressed and emotional. Frank rocket-launches out of his window of tolerance and is no longer able to listen or reflect properly. He can no longer empathise with the other, but fights, flees or freezes.

In her childhood, Gizella often felt abandoned and was often abandoned by friends as well. She lives with the negative core, though: I will always be abandoned again, I don't matter. When Mustafa does not respond to her questions and e-mails, this core thought is triggered and evokes intense emotional reactions.

These parents react from their survival reaction and fight, flee or freeze: the destructive patterns are active again, parents are caught in them, and the children are caught in the middle.

Learning to de-escalate and calm down in time is therefore an important point of interest. Parents who learn to recognise the destructive patterns and emotional escalations can stop these patterns and

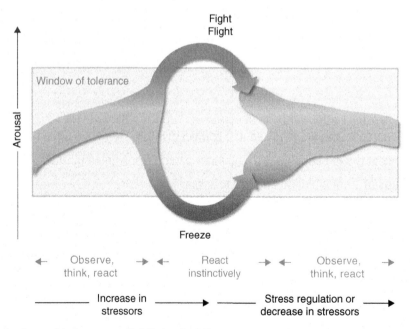

Figure 6 The window of tolerance © Niels de Nies

first calm down before taking action. They may, for instance, first ask what the other person means. They can postpone their reaction and first consider calmly how they want to react. In this way, they can make sure that a safe environment is created for their children, so that they do not have to carry the same painful experiences with them. This is an important motive for learning to calm down in time and to stay connected.

After we have explained how you can understand that conflicts keep getting out of hand, and what that has to do with how unpleasant experiences are stored in your body and mind and how you react when tensions increase, we ask you to think about your own window of tolerance.

The vulnerability cycle

The fact that conflicts sometimes persist has to do with the fact that parents trigger each other and hit a painful spot in each other. And that makes that you start to fight (get angry), flee (get scared) or freeze (block), each in your own way. This is a survival strategy (SS) in response to triggers, a vulnerability (V). That is why, in this context, we also refer to 'the vulnerability cycle' (see Figure 7).

If Lewis is afraid that he doesn't matter, that no one bothers about him, when he feels excluded (his vulnerability), he will rocket-launch into his survival strategy: get angry, call to let know that he is there, chase. Lilian feels overwhelmed by Lewis's anger and chasing; she launches into her survival strategy by withdrawing and freezing. You can also look at this situation the other way around. Lilian is afraid that Lewis will be angry and withdraws, which triggers Lewis, who feels unimportant and gets angry. These are vicious patterns without a specific beginning or end.

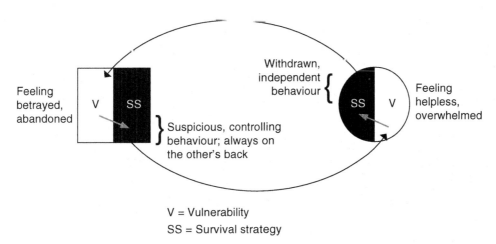

Figure 7 The vulnerability cycle (Scheinkman & Fishbane, 2007)

Comprehensive assignment 2a

What vulnerabilities and triggers do you recognise in yourself?

My vulnerabilities or sensitivities are:

_____

_____

_____

_____

My triggers are:

_____

_____

_____

_____

My reactions (survival strategies) are:

_____

_____

_____

Also ask the people around you what vulnerabilities, triggers and reactions they recognise in themselves and in you. Write them down below.

_____

_____

_____

Comprehensive assignment 2b

When was the last time you were very angry at the other parent or got very emotional or anxious? Can you link that incident to this theory? Can you, for instance, draw your own vulnerability cycle? And understand and accept yourself in it? And perhaps also see that the other person reacts to vulnerability too?

Draw your own vulnerability cycle here (look at the example in appendix 2).

Comprehensive assignment 2c

Study your own reactions

Watch your own reactions in the coming days and consider how sensitive you are to certain actions or reactions from others.

Consider:

- when you are no longer able to regulate your emotions;
- when you manage to calm yourself down and stay out of the destructive patterns.

Calming down

You cannot always avoid being hurt by what someone else does, says or does not do. However, you can learn to postpone your reaction, to calm down in time and to calm yourself down. If you notice that you get tensed up, consider what you can do to calm down. Some people distract themselves by doing something, or they listen to music to calm down. Others seek support from a person they trust, or they retreat and need to be alone for a while.

Do you know what calms you down?

Comprehensive assignment 3

What calms me down?

I calm down when

___

___

___

or by

___

___

___

Comprehensive assignment 4

Exercise in delayed response

A delayed reaction means actively refraining from action. A helpful thought could be: I don't necessarily have to react immediately, I can do so later too.

Actively refraining from reacting can help to:

- avoid an impulsive reaction (count to ten);
- avoid being tempted to do something that you will regret later on;
- give yourself the time to do something that will keep you out of the destructive pattern;
- prevent a situation from escalating;
- keep the peace so that you can think clearly again;
- take the time to think about what a possible reaction means for your child;
- let go and accept that you don't have control of everything except your own behaviour.

In the coming week, I will train myself to not take immediate action.

I resolve to:

___

Comprehensive assignment 5

Give an example of the past week when the stress increased and you managed to calm down in time and stay within your window of tolerance.

___

What did your children notice? And what did you notice about the children when you succeeded?

___

Ask people in your network if they can think of something that calms you down or helps you.

___

Write it down here.

> **Mother**: My mother told me that she remembered from the past that I would calm down if I had listened to music in my room for a while.

> **Father**: When I asked my current partner, she laughed and said: 'You just have to run for a while. You are a completely different person after that.'

> **Mother**: My sister immediately knew what I meant and told me that I needed to have no one around me for a while.

> **Father**: My friend told me that going outside and around the block with the dog makes him calm. Then I thought, 'I could do that too.'

Homework for session 5

 ## Purpose of the homework

The purpose of the homework for this session is to practice a different way of reacting that could help you get out of the destructive pattern. Many parents wonder what they can do if the other person doesn't change. You have absolutely no control over what the other person does or says. What you can do is change your own reaction to the other person's behaviour. You can influence that.

 ## Assignment 5.1

Read: explanation illusion of control.

Illusion of control

Some divorced parents find it difficult to find a new balance in their relationship with the other parent. Often, there are still issues that cause tensions – tensions that make them stay caught together in destructive communication patterns. These kinds of patterns, we know, are the enemy of relationships and therefore of good cooperation as parents. They make good intentions invisible because distrust and suspicion become dominant. The hope that one day something will change decreases, and the feeling of powerlessness increases.

To get out of this seemingly hopeless position, parents look for solutions. Two reactions are often heard:

1. You try to change the other person so that they do what you want them to do, for instance by exerting pressure, making demands, going to court, prescribing behaviour, imposing your will . . .
2. You do not want to meet the other person, for instance by ignoring or avoiding the other or by refusing to cooperate, avoiding issues or frustrating the other . . .

The risk is that, in this way, the differences between the two parents will be magnified and that the behaviour of the other will be experienced only as hostile and regarded increasingly as unacceptable. The patterns continue to be fed in this way, and there is a danger that issues will not settle down and will even escalate. This can lead to a cycle of (emotional) violence.

Letting go of the illusion of control

There is another way. That other way is based on the fundamental awareness that we cannot force another person to do something if they themselves do not agree, whether it be a relative, a friend, an employee, a child or an ex-partner. We cannot demand that someone else stop doing something that we want to stop if they do not cooperate. The idea that it is in our power to impose our will on someone else is called 'the illusion of control.'

What is possible is that we shift the attention from the other person's behaviour to our own attitude and our own behaviour. We can decide to relate differently to something the other person does or says which we disapprove of, which we fear or which gives us a sense of injustice. When we figure out what we can do differently ourselves, we give up 'the illusion of control'! Then we stop trying to control the other person's life. This creates space for the other person, and at the same time we can free ourselves from the other person's (attempts to) control over us. By acting this way, you break the cycle of hostility, control and the mutual dependence on the other person's cooperation. And no matter how contradictory it may sound, this increases the chance of 'good enough' cooperation as parents.

An experiment!

It is not easy shifting from the focus on the other to the focus on yourself. Besides, doing something else requires a lot of practice, effort and perseverance. If you succeed in changing your own reactions, the outcome will most likely be that the continuous pattern will be broken and that you will feel less powerless, even if nothing has changed yet in the behaviour of the other person. The sense of control will increase, but rather with respect to your own life and your own actions. Letting go also has to do with *really* separating (see appendix 3).

To make real letting go a success, the most important ingredient is that you yourself no longer continue with the ongoing arguments and stop behaving in a way that can be experienced as provocative or even threatening by the other person. This is crucial and essential! It means: no more threatening, shouting, making hateful remarks, provoking, making accusations, speaking ill of the other, stalking, ignoring or avoiding the other, blaming, frustrating – in short, everything that you yourself wouldn't want to see happen to you either. This is incredibly difficult because it is so counter-intuitive. It often feels like giving in or giving up. If this exercise in self-control is difficult for you, the following mantra may help: 'strike while the iron is cold.' This means that in every situation you can choose to delay your reaction and come back to something later, but with a calmed mind. It is not about winning, it is about persevering. This creates peace and space for yourself and for the children. This requires self-control, practice and perseverance.

A second important ingredient is that you do not 'demonise' the other person. Demonising means that you cannot see the good in the other parent anymore. You become more and more convinced, as it were, that the other person is only trying to frustrate you. Beautiful moments you once shared disappear in the background, and you do not see, or you ignore, exceptions to the belief that the other has only bad intentions. With the best will in the world, you can no longer think of positive things about the other parent, and if you ask the people close to you, they sometimes do not know what to say either. This in turn strengthens your idea that the other parent is no good at all.

Instead of seeing everything as deliberate, intentional negative behaviour towards you (and your children), it helps to choose to see the other as a parent who makes different choices in parenting and has a different view of what is good for the children, without qualifying this as 'wrong' or 'bad.' As mentioned before, the middle ground of 'good enough' parenting is far preferable to an endless conflict over who does best. This, too, is better achieved with a calm mind.

A third important ingredient is that you ask for help from the people around you – your relatives, friends, current partner – to support you and to persevere. It is important to tell them what you resolved and to 'coach' them, like you, not to blame anymore, not to react immediately if you feel something is unfair, and to keep the calm. You ask for their support to help you sustain this new way of reacting for a long time.

During this experiment, it is important that you stay friendly and respectful towards the other parent and the people in his/her network. Children told us that all these seemingly small gestures, such as 'greeting instead of looking away', 'being kind instead of grumpy' and 'being nice instead of reacting curtly', are felt, noticed and experienced as pleasant by them.

Assignment 5.2
Influence–no influence

Now make a list of things that you can influence and a list of things that you cannot influence but may be stressful for you.

I have *no* influence on: I *do* have influence on:

Now focus on the list of things that you can influence. Choose a number of things that you will practice in the coming week.

_____

_____

_____

What changes will your children notice?

_____

_____

_____

What do you think this means for them?

_____

_____

_____

Writing a letter

By writing a letter to the other parent, you can let him or her know what you have decided. In that letter, you tell him or her what you are going to do differently from now on. Writing this letter requires some preparation, though.

The preparation consists of three steps:

1. Start with a task that focuses on everything you can influence yourself without depending on others. On a sheet of paper write your intentions what you are going to do differently. -> Look at the first ingredient: focusing on myself and stopping my own escalating behavior.
2. Next, make a list of situations which bother you the most, how you react to them now and what you could do differently in the future. Remember once again that you cannot break a vicious cycle by constantly pointing at the other person. You can only break a vicious cycle by reacting differently yourself.
3. Finally, figure out which situations are really important or have priority, and which matters can wait or do not deserve any attention. You decide not to be bothered by them anymore. You remain unaffected by them, or you count to ten. Maybe one day you will be able to pay attention to these matters again, but right now they are not important.

Discuss these three steps also with the people around you, your partner, relatives, friends and other loved ones. It is important to tell them that you are doing this for the children, to create a different, relaxed space between their parents, and that they can help by doing the same thing and by moving with you. Surely, they can help you with this.

Structure of the letter

Now you are ready to write the letter. Your letter consists of five parts, five paragraphs:

1. You start your letter with what you value about the other person as a mother/father (this is in line with the assignment for the fourth session, the one with the symbols).
2. You then write down what you are not going to do anymore and what you do intend to do in relation to the other person. These are the things that you can influence, that you can choose yourself, out of respect for the other as a parent of the children.
3. Then you write down how you are going to relate differently to the things that you cannot directly influence. So you write down what you have decided to do differently, in the realisation that you cannot change the other person and cannot prescribe how he or she is to behave.
4. Mention the people you have asked for support to help you and to persevere in not trying to change the other person anymore.
5. End your letter by saying that you hope that there will be opportunities again in the future to be present together at moments that are important to the children, and that you would like to believe that it will be possible to raise the children in a healthy way (even though you are different and have different ideas about parenting).

Example of the structure of a letter (with example sentences)

Dear . . .

What I appreciate about you as a father/mother . . .

What I am happy about when it comes to the kids is that you . . .

The kids are lucky to have you as a father/mother, because . . .

Things, however, are not always going well between us. I want to do everything I can to change that. I know that I often . . . (behaviour).

I resolve not to do that again. I won't . . . anymore. And I won't . . . anymore (accuse you, prescribe behaviour, grumble at you, be unkind, etc.).

What I am going to do is . . . (things which you know the other person appreciates and which the children consider 'normal' behaviour for parents).

So I have decided that I will continue to greet you, that I will be friendly with you, that I will speak about you with respect to the children. I won't overload you with messages either. I will only send you an SMS or WhatsApp message if the situation requires so.

I cannot force you to take care of the division of holidays, to return the children on time, to listen to your voicemail and respond to it, to have the children come to my birthday, to not call me anymore, to not start any more proceedings. I cannot demand that you apply the same rules as I do and that you raise the children in exactly the same way as I wish you would do. I have decided that I do not want to feel so powerless about this anymore and I will react differently from now on.

I have resolved to stop arguing. If I have a question or a request, I will let you know. Whether you respond or not, I will leave that with you. If I want to pass something on, I will let you know by calling, sending an e-mail or, if necessary, sending a letter or leaving a letter in your letterbox. Whether you decide to answer the phone, to read the messages or the letter is not up to me, but at least I will have informed you.

I have also decided to set your letters/mails aside if they contain threatening or compelling language. I will respond, however, to regular mails from you about practical arrangements. What I am not prepared to do is to accept that you or your lawyer forbid me to watch my children play sports when it is your weekend. However, I have decided that I choose not to do it anymore if this causes extra tension for the children. This means that I can decide to be absent on other occasions too, for the sake of the children, if you say that my presence with you causes tensions.

I sincerely hope that, in the future, we will be able to attend activities of our children together again, especially when it concerns special events such as a graduation, but I realise that this will take time.

I will inform the people around me and the children about my decisions. I will ask them to support me in this so that I will persevere.

I believe that we are able to raise our children in a healthy way without living under one roof, without arguing, by dealing with each other in a calm and quiet way.

 ## Assignment 5.3
Write a letter using the above explanation.

Assignment 5.4

Mail an assignment that you have set for yourself to the therapists of the parent group at least one week before the next meeting. What do you want to practice to improve the situation for the children? This can be anything as long as it is something that you can influence yourself. For instance: I am going to make sure that I stay in touch with the other person. This is possible because you can influence this yourself. A bad example would be: I am going to wait until the other person treats me with respect. This is not possible because you have no influence on that.

Assignment 5.5

Writing a letter (exercise)

Write a letter using the aforementioned explanation.

GROUP THERAPY FOR HIGH-CONFLICT DIVORCE

Homework for session 6

Purpose of the homework

It is important that you decide for yourself what you want to practise from now on in order to continue to make progress.

You will get greater insight into which of the people around you strengthen the positive stories about the other parent and which strengthen the negative stories. Positive stories about the other parent make it easier for your child, and negative stories make it more difficult. Even though your child can sometimes express him- or herself very negatively about one parent.

Current partners and stepparents have an important role but often find themselves in a difficult position. Especially for them, there is an assignment where they are given tools on how to support the process of you and your child.

This homework will prepare you for the presentation you will give to your child in session 7.

Assignment 6.1

Send an e-mail to the therapists this week in which you write what you want to practise in the next two weeks.

Positive things

Assignment 6.2a

In session 4, you said positive things about the other parent and heard positive things about yourself. How was it like to express them and to receive them?

Write that down.

_____

_____

_____

_____

Stand in the shoes of your child and think of what your child would like to hear from you about the other parent. Write that down.

_____

_____

_____

Can you also recall a positive memory of you as parents and your child?

_____

_____

_____

> **Margie (mother)**: I really did my best to think of something, but I just couldn't. And my mother didn't know anything and I needn't bother asking my brother. It may sound stupid, but then I asked the soccer trainer. And he knew something. And when he said that Peter can be so funny and make the children laugh, especially when they are very tense before a game, I suddenly knew something I like about him as a father.

> **Reyan (father)**: I didn't find it difficult to think of something, but I noticed that I found it difficult to say it. I could hardly get it out of my mouth. Then I asked my father to say something positive about her to me in front of the children and all I did was agree. The children then started to beam.

> **Rina (mother)**: My daughter is sixteen years old. She asked if I was feeling well and if everything was okay when I said something positive about her father. You should have seen that face. We had a real good laugh about that. But it was also confronting. That she really doesn't expect that from me anymore.

> **Rickie (5 years old)**: During the break, my father said 'Thank you' to my mother. That made me feel happy.

> **Sophia (14)**: Really ridiculous. Suddenly my mother starts saying all kinds of positive things about my father. As if I can't figure that out . . . Really stupid . . .

> **Sebastian (11 years old)**: I had baked cookies with my mother and her friend. And my father said that he appreciated that and that he liked the cookies.

 ### Assignment 6.2b

Say something positive about the other parent to your child once or twice in the next two weeks, or to someone else in front of your child.

How did your child react?

_____

_____

_____

We know that there are also children who are angry with the other parent, or disappointed, and talk very negatively about the other parent. Don't confirm your child in those negative thoughts. Say something positive about the other parent now and then.

Ask your partner, relatives or friends for help if you cannot think of anything positive about the other parent. Children of parents who cannot think of positive things about each other grow up in a black-and-white world, where one person is completely good and the other is completely bad. This can make it difficult for them in future relationships. After all, every relationship has more and less positive sides.

Assignment 6.3

Check your network

To what extent do the people around you support or stimulate you in the change you are going through for the children's sake? With the following assignment, you can figure that out for yourself.

Answer the following questions:

Which people are important to you?

_____

_____

In what way do you receive support from them now?

_____

_____

Do they also support you in your attempts to no longer express yourself so negatively about the other parent?

_____

_____

Which people are important sources of support for your child(ren)? How do they support a positive change?

_____

_____

_____

Letter from children to their network

The children in the children's group are also working on a letter for the important people around you.

Dear grandparents, grandmothers, aunts, uncles, neighbours, friends, relatives and current partners of our parents,

We were in the No Kids in the Middle programme. And our parents too. Our parents worked hard to stop the fighting. In the children's group we received a lot of support from each other and we also shared and did a lot together. We also want to share something with you. You are important to us and our parents.

There is already a beautiful letter in which children tell how they feel. This letter is addressed to all divorced parents of the Netherlands and was written by children of Villa Pinedo.

We have now written a letter to the network of all divorced parents, so for you. In this letter we would like to explain and ask you a number of things. We wrote the letter together on a flip-chart during the last meeting of the children's group. The children's therapists helped to put it together. This is the result.

Letter to our network:

Having divorced parents has its advantages. For example, we go on vacation twice;-)

It is also nice to be read twice. And there is more peace in the house. Besides, if we have an argument with one of them, there is still the other one.

Still, we often feel torn between the two parents we love. You will probably have noticed how difficult and tense it has become.

But you can help!

SO: May we ask you a few things:

Will you please be nice to both our parents and will you act the same to us and our parents as you did before the divorce?

Will you please not fight and be nice to each other?

Will you please not talk badly about each other and not say stupid things to each other?

Will you please be friends?

Will you help so that we can have fun together?

We would like to let you know that it doesn't feel good when our parents and you are fighting.

And if our parents do argue, will you help us to think about something else and do nice things with us?

Will you please encourage us when we don't feel like going to our mum or dad?

And stepparents, will you please let our parents decide for themselves and not interfere too much. Then I will be happier and it will be more chill. Then I will have more fun with you too.

Will you please not talk or shout when I am on the phone with my mum or dad?

We want to thank you for the help you have already given,

Love,
On behalf of all the children.

For the new partner

Many children who participate in No Kids in the Middle have to deal with a new partner of their father and/or mother. This can go very well, but it can also cause a lot of tension for the new partner and the child.

The new partner/stepparent is very important to the child. The many conversations with new partners and/or stepparents show time and again how much difference they can make in a child's life. Children of stepparents also have to deal with a new situation. A lot will change for them too, the impact of which can be felt in different ways in the mutual relationships within the newly formed family.

Sometimes things go very well. The 'chemistry' between stepparent and child is good and they tune in to each other. Then a stepparent can be a source of support for children. And stepbrothers and sisters can also be of help to each other. However, if the exes argue a lot, there can also be a lot of tension in the new relationship.

Stepparents/current partners all too often face many dilemmas, issues that they have never thought about before. They feel that they have suddenly ended up in a situation that they could not have properly comprehended beforehand. They want to help, are trying to figure out their position, have a feeling that they have limited influence and are often confronted with feelings of powerlessness, especially if the tensions persist.

You may recognise the following situations:

- As a stepparent, you may feel you are in a difficult position with regard to your partner's child. The child may reject you, no matter how much time and attention you put into building a relationship. Sometimes you get the impression that the other parent does not allow the child to build a positive relationship with you.
- As a stepparent, you may run into parenting issues. Do you have to correct a child or not? And if so, how? A child may not accept it if you correct it.
- As a stepparent, you may notice that your partner changes completely as soon as his or her own children arrive and that there is little room or attention for you, or for your children. It may bother you a lot if the other parent shuts you out or treats you unfairly.

You can probably add more situations to this list yourself.

There are also new issues for parents and children:

- When there are many tensions between your children and your new partner, you may feel caught between them. You want to support your children, but your current partner too. And if you side with your children, your partner may get angry and vice versa.
- As a parent, you may feel caught between the wishes or rules of your current partner regarding the raising of your child and that of the other parent. The same applies to the stepparent who has a certain expectation of you when it comes to how you treat his or her children.
- As a parent, you may feel very frustrated and powerless when you notice that the other parent's current partner is approaching your children or yourself in a way that puts your children in a difficult position.
- A child may feel caught if it likes the stepparent, but cannot form a positive relationship with him or her because the other parent would regard that as betrayal.
- It becomes very difficult for a child if the stepparent speaks badly of the other parent. The child wants to defend the other parent, but may feel that it is not allowed to. Many children start to feel guilty in such a situation.
- A child may have great difficulty with new rules from the stepparent. For instance, from unlimited gaming to only one hour a day.

These are all examples of situations you may face.

Switching moments

It is difficult for children, parents and stepparents to tack between all the switching moments during the week. Moments of being together as partners without children are alternated with moments that one of the parent's children are there, and with moments that the other parent's children are there, but also with moments that the children of both parents are there. This requires a lot of switching from partnership to parenting to stepparenting, and to moments when one is in the role of parent and the other in the role of partner. Switching moments can cause confusion and tension, especially if the other parent interferes. It gets really difficult for the children when the adults often disagree about the rules and agreements. When parents argue a lot, it is sometimes difficult for the children to build a relationship with the stepparent. On the other hand, a stepparent can be a confidant too.

Assignment 6.4a

How do your partner and the people around you talk to you and/or your children about the parenting of the other parent? State who strengthens the positive stories and who strengthens the negative ones.

_____

_____

_____

Assignment 6.4b

For current partners and stepparents:

Because many stepparents, parents and children feel stuck, here is an assignment for the current partners and stepparents. If you were present at the network evening, you may have already understood that the children are central to this project. This is also the case in the next exercise.

During the network evening, we explained that in this project there is a lot of emphasis on involving the current partners. Do you feel that you are well aware of what is happening in the group and what your partner is working on? If not, ask about it yourself. In the preceding sections you have read about the issues stepparents may run into. Do you recognise any of them? Where do you run into yourself?

_____

_____

_____

_____

Maybe we haven't emphasised enough yet that stepparents are often very valuable to children. Especially when they are not directly involved in the conflict, they can have a calming effect on the parent/partner and on the children. We often see that the new partner/the stepparent is very helpful in reducing the conflict and finding other ways to deal with the differences of opinion.

If you could see yourself from a distance, what would you see? Can you help de-escalate the conflict? How do you do that?

_____

_____

_____

Do you ever disagree with your partner about the children? What do you argue about, and how does that go?

_____

_____

_____

Now put yourself in the child's position and look through his or her eyes at you and your behaviour. What could a child feel and experience?

_____

_____

_____

If there are reactions that make it difficult for the child, talk to your partner and the people from the network about how you could change your reactions so that the child will feel less stuck. Write down what you have come up with.

_____

_____

_____

We have understood from many new partners/stepparents how difficult it can be in your position. New partners/stepparents also have to deal with feelings of frustration and powerlessness. You may think that the other parent and his or her partner need to change. Maybe you are right. But you have also noticed that you have no influence on that. Reading appendices 1 to 3 may help you deal with complex situations. These appendices are about learning to tolerate situations and to deal with them in a different way so that it can be done, and it helps to get the children out of the middle.

If there is something you think needs to be discussed, talk about it with your partner and, if desired, ask if he/she will make an appointment with the therapists. This can also help.

Finally, stepparents can contribute a lot to reducing the conflict by:

- not going along with negative stories about the other parent;
- saying something positive about the other parent;
- being prepared to adapt to what the children are used to;
- doing fun things with the children (especially those you like yourself!);
- not pushing the other to talk, working on a good relationship, leaving space;
- having patience and stamina, as this is almost always rewarded.

Letter from children of Villa Pinedo to new partners

We were monsters. My sister and I. Terrible little monsters. My father had a hard time, because we complained that we wanted to go home, that it wasn't fun to be with him, especially when his girlfriend was around.

My father and my stepmother at the time once had the courage to take us on holidays: three weeks in France. As it turned out, we went home earlier. It was the first and last holiday we spent together. We weren't easy on them. How? Actually by doing mean little things. Tormenting, laughing at them, making stupid remarks, frustrating them, nagging, wanting to go home . . . What should have been a nice, beautiful holiday, eventually turned into a tragedy on a French campsite. I think that after this vacation they badly needed to go on a real vacation . . .

Years later, actually only a few weeks ago, it dawned on me what kind of monsters we were. My ex-stepmother told me how we were, how mean, how difficult. My father and my stepmother have broken up, too, and yet she can say: 'Your father did everything for you and you didn't see that. Why did you do that?'

Now that I think about it myself and look back: yes, we were monsters. How that came about? It's quite simple: a conflict of loyalty. I couldn't like my stepmother, because I thought I would lose my mother if I did. I couldn't have a nice time with Dad, because I would have to tell my mother. And my mother thought my father was terrible. I felt I couldn't like my father, because I lived with my mother and things had to stay nice and cosy at home. What would happen if I stood up for my father? If I would say it had been super fun with dad? That I missed him and wanted to go to him? Would it still be liveable and nice at home? Or would there be constant arguments?

It is now very easy for me to explain how I felt back then, what kind of dilemmas I had to deal with. But at the time, I didn't realise. I was surviving and making sure I had a home where the atmosphere was okay and safe. To realise this later is confronting. I've done things and said things I am not proud of. And all that as a result of the divorce. You could say: you were brainwashed. And yes, I really was.

I am deliberately writing this in the past tense. Because now I know how it works. I can look at the situation with much more distance. My father was a good father and he tried a lot. I can see why I reacted like that and I know what I felt then. I am still not proud of it, but I can feel peace when I realise that it all happened under the influence of what was going on. And that it can be different; a positive influence, so that children are not brainwashed but can feel at home with both parents, where they can and may have a good time with both of them. That is what I wish for every child. And parents can too. Make sure, and let it show in your behaviour, that your child is free to go to the other parent and to love the other parent. To have a good time there. And to miss the other parent.

Yvette (24 years old)

Presentations by parents to children

We ask all parents to make a presentation for the children about themselves, as a parent, about what they have learned and want to change or work on to make it different for the children in the future. The presentation will be given no sooner than in session 7, but maybe you want to know already what the purpose is, so you can think about it. You may decide for yourself what you want to make.

The children look very much forward to what their parents have thought up and made for them. It is very exciting for them. Parents also find it exciting.

Here we give some examples. Make sure that a presentation does not take more than five minutes in total.

- A father had made a poem.
- A mother brought a backpack filled with bricks that represented the weight of the burden that children had to carry for years because of the arguments and tension between the parents. During

the presentation she removed the stones from the bag and filled it with cards, each with a wish for the future and a promise what she would do her best for.
- A father told a story about two symbols he had brought.
- A mother had made a PowerPoint presentation about before and after No Kids in the Middle.
- There are parents who do something with music or with photos. Others are very creative with paper, glue, paint and all kinds of materials or they show a short film and tell something about it. One parent showed a YouTube video with a song by a popular singer about his children growing up.

What we do not want is a presentation in which you, as a parent, tell your children how great they are, what they are good at, what you are proud of, that they are the best children in the world and that you will always fight for them. That is a presentation about the children, and that is not the purpose of the presentation. Fortunately, the children know this already. They are especially curious about what you have learned in this project and what you want to change about the tensions between you as parents. Like the father who said: 'I won't talk so negatively about your mother anymore. I know now what it is like for you, because she is still your mother.'

The parent presentations are impressive for both the own and the other children. Children see the vulnerability of the parents and deal with it in a caring way. They find it very exciting to see what their parents have come up with, what they have made especially for them. They are curious about the resolution, no matter how small, their parents come up with.

We know from previous group meetings that the presentations are very different and that parents always appear to be vulnerable and longing for more peace and better times, and that they want to work to make that happen. That is nice to see. If you want to use the projector for a film or a presentation, let us know well in advance so that we can arrange for the necessary equipment. We would like to receive films and presentations from you in advance.

We believe that each of you will be able to show what you have learned in the past period in a presentation. Don't forget to ask the people from your network for help. They may also want to add an element to your presentation; for instance, about what they have changed and how they want to continue to support the children in the future.

The children's presentations

During the next session (session 6), the children will present something to the parents and therapists. They have all prepared something in which they show how they experience being a child of parents in conflict. They have prepared a text, a drawing or a film, they made music or something else.

The children find it exciting to show their presentations to the parents. They show only what they want to show. Still, they will be alert: How will mum and dad react? Will they be angry or sad, or will they laugh?

What the children show is what they have thought of themselves. The therapists supervised the process and did not influence the content of their presentation. It is the child's voice!

Think in advance about how you can keep it safe enough for all children. This is important and actually speaks for itself. We emphasise it here because sometimes children can show something which may give you as a parent something of a shock, which may be painful to hear or which makes you want to react immediately. After the children's presentations, parents and therapists leave the room of the children's group, and there is time to discuss and exchange experiences and feelings.

Actually, it always goes well. Usually parents are very impressed. And so are the therapists.

GROUP THERAPY FOR HIGH-CONFLICT DIVORCE

Homework for session 7

 ### Purpose of the homework

Session 7 is the session in which the parents present what they have learned in the project and what they wish for their children in the future. You will finish that presentation. We are also approaching the end of the group programme.

We hope that you have gained greater insight into things that can be changed and things that cannot be changed. That you resign yourself to what we call 'the tragedy of life.' And that you learn to deal with things that cannot be changed in a way that keeps the children out of the middle. Especially that you cannot change the other person.

> Father to another father in the group who complains about the behaviour of his ex: 'There is no sense in it, I understand that now. You are not going to be able to change the other person. So you have a problem. And you will have to deal with that.'

The final preparations for your presentation

Involve your network. We appreciate it when you inform the therapists in advance about what you're going to do and if you need a laptop or projector or something else. Make sure your presentation does not take more than five minutes, so all parents will get a chance. If you have any questions about your presentation, you can always send an e-mail to the therapists.

We would like to share the following thoughts/consideration with you about single parenthood. You have probably heard many times that people divorce as partners, not as parents, and that you should continue to work and communicate well as a parent team. You have no doubt tried that, but it did not work out. Sometimes there are so many differences between parents, and there have been so many painful and hurtful experiences, that communicating and working together as parents always lead to rising tensions. Since basically every parent wants to be a good parent, you will feel guilty if you do not succeed, while everyone says how important it is for the children. And still you feel that you are doing everything right, that you do not know what you could do even better. And automatically you will put the blame with the other person. Every time you are asked to cooperate – by the court, by social workers, by others – the tensions and problems seem to increase rather than decrease.

If this happens, it is often better to first distance yourself from the other, to let go of each other, to work as divorced parents, also referred to as *parallel parenting*. This means that communication is kept to a minimum and sometimes goes through a trusted person, for instance a brother with whom both parents have contact. Or, if there are no people anymore who have contact with both parents, each of you may also ask a contact person, a buddy from your own network, to function as a 'letterbox.' The contacts are then channelled through them. The two buddies have contact with each other and, if necessary, discuss solutions which they pass on to the parents. In this way, the children will not become the messengers, because they shouldn't.

Single parenthood also means that you let go, that you are no longer so preoccupied with what the other person does with the children. That you realise that there are big differences, but that you accept that now because you cannot change the other person anyway. And children learn to live with the parents they have, just like parents learn to live with the children they have.

Only if parents demonstrably abuse and damage their child is this different. Then, you cannot let go. But these parents are not enrolled for our No Kids in the Middle project. We work only with parents who are good enough for their children.

So we don't ask you to improve communication by consulting a lot with each other. If that is possible in a relaxed atmosphere, that is fine. But if this causes tensions time and again, communication can be improved by leaving each other alone and focusing on your own life with and without your children. Then there will be more space and peace for everyone. Then you can move on with your lives.

Issues

After the break there will be time to work on your own issues again. Think about what issue you could bring up.

'My ex always wants to determine everything and he is always against everything. So, there is no way I could change the parenting arrangements. Now, the children will not be able to attend my parents' 50th wedding anniversary.'

'My ex-wife never bothered about her family during our marriage. Now, she suddenly wants the children to go to her parents' wedding anniversary, where I had booked a weekend in Barcelona with them.'

'Every time the children come back, they look like a bunch of tramps. They haven't taken a shower, their hair hasn't been combed, no clean clothes. They are just plain dirty. We have to teach them how to look after themselves, don't we?'

Assignment 7.1

These are examples of issues parents bring up to work on with each other. Have you brought up an issue yet? If you look at the issues mentioned, where would you see openings?

_____

_____

_____

Assignment 7.2

Draw a comic strip (optional)

You can draw a comic strip about an issue: what do you disagree about? How do the children feel about it? First you let the story end badly. Things get completely out of hand. What happens to the children? And with you as parents? And with the people around you? Then let the story end in such a way that you work it out. How does that look like? How do the children react? And the people around you?

GROUP THERAPY FOR
HIGH-CONFLICT DIVORCE

Homework for session 8

 ## Purpose of the homework

Now you have to turn the messages given by the children in the presentations and your own presentation into actions in daily life. Focus on what you can change, regardless of what the other parent does or does not do.

Evaluation

The next session is the eighth and last group meeting. This session will be dedicated to evaluation. In preparation for the evaluation, think about the following: When did you manage to stay out of the destructive patterns for the sake of your child, and when didn't you? And why was that?

_____

_____

_____

_____

What skills or traits helped you in these situations? (See 'Traits and skills', page 87).

_____

_____

_____

How do you manage to allow positive stories about the parenting of the other parent?

_____

_____

Have you managed to make positive remarks about the other parent to your child(ren) or to make them to someone from the network in front of your child? Provide an example:

_____

_____

_____

What helps you to do so?

_____

_____

_____

When doesn't it work, and how come?

_____

_____

_____

Have you managed to give up the illusion of being able to change the other parent?

_____

How does that show up?

_____

_____

What do the children notice when you manage to do so?

_____

_____

Do you notice in your children that they develop relationally and that they can see both parents as people with good sides and not-so-good sides? Describe how you notice.

_____

_____

_____

When are you able to reconcile with the past and with the other parent for the sake of your child(ren)'s development? And when aren't you?

_____

_____

_____

What does that have to do with?

_____

_____

_____

Do your children have more peace in their lives? How has that come about?

_____

_____

_____

What has been your part in that, and how do you feel about that?

_____

_____

What would your next step be, with your child(ren) in mind, to stop the destructive pattern and to stay out of it?

_____

_____

During the evaluation there is also room for critical notes. As you have noticed while reading the workbook, your ideas and experiences are very important to us. We will discuss this with you by asking you the following two questions:

- What should we stick to?
- What should we do differently?

Assignment 8.1

What can you do differently? What can you change in your behaviour after hearing the children's messages?

Fill in Figure 8. Start with the children's field. So, suppose that an important message from the children was that they want parents to 'just be civil again.' Then you write down in the children's field: 'They

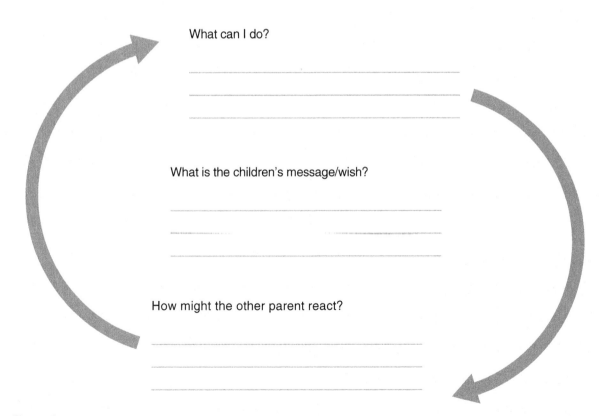

Figure 8 What I do (2)

see us being nice to each other.' And then write down in your own field what you can do to make this possible for your children. Finally, write down what the other parent's reaction to this could be.

What can I do?

_____

_____

_____

What is the children's message/wish?

_____

_____

_____

How might the other parent react?

_____

_____

_____

Additional explanation

Suppose your child gave the following message during the presentation: 'I would like my parents to be normal/nice to each other.' This is a wish that has been expressed in many presentations. You can then write down in the children's field: 'Wants us to be nice to each other.' Then think about what you can do to make that happen and write that down in the field: 'What can I do?' For instance: 'I say hello when he/she comes to pick up the children and I say goodbye when he/she leaves.' Finally, write down how the other parent might react to that. In a number of cases, parents wrote down: 'Treats me with respect, too.' Children notice such changes immediately and tell each other about it in the children's group.

It may be that your child has given a message in the presentation that is more negative about the other parent than about you. For instance: 'I feel happy with one parent, confused with the other.' Even then, you can write down in the children's field: 'Wants to feel less confused.' Then think about what you can do about it and write that down in your own field. Now, you may think: there's nothing I can do about that. This is something for the other to work on. This is understandable. Still, we have learned something different from parents who previously participated in No Kinds in the Middle. A mother, for instance, decided to stop evaluating the weekend with dad with her daughter for an hour. But most of all, she decided to motivate her daughter to discuss with her father what made her so confused.

Maybe you think 'That's a no-go, the other won't listen to that,' or 'she has already tried that, it doesn't help a thing.' Perhaps you are right about that. Yet, it is good to do it. Just take another look at the explanation about letting go and the illusion of control on pages XX and XX. We count on you to realise at this stage of the therapy that you have no influence on the other parent's behaviour. You can do your utmost to follow your children's messages and be nice to the other parent. This does not mean that the other person will, by definition, be nice to you too.

Is that bad? No, it is not. If you do things differently, it means half as much stress for your children (see appendix 2). Ask for support from your network to be able to continue your new actions for the sake of the children. This is really difficult, but certainly not impossible.

Read the following statements from a parent, a child and someone from the network.

> **Jason**: During the presentations, my son and daughter showed a video in which they acted that they are so troubled by the tension when I walk them to their mother's front door, where I thought this was very important to them. I understand now that they find it very annoying. I've talked to them about it and now I drop them off at the corner and I let their mother know why I do this.

> **Jody's grandmother**: My daughter came to me, terribly upset. She said: 'Finally, I got the courage to take a step and start a chat with him at the soccer field . . . then he turns around and pretends not to see me. Now, a lot of good that will do the kids.' I gave her a cup of tea and told her I was proud of her. Of course, I would rather give him a kick in the pants. But nothing good will come of that.

> **Jody tells in the children's group**: I was having soccer practice and suddenly I saw my parents standing side by side. And they didn't even get into an argument. It made me miss a ball. But then I scored and they both cheered. I only had to look in one direction and not think about who to look at first.

Assignment 8.2

Changing something in your behaviour

Over the next two weeks, try to change your own behaviour in response to the children's messages during the presentations.

What are you going to try?

___

___

___

How did it go?

___

___

___

What do you think your children will notice?

___

___

___

What reaction did you see in your children?

_____

_____

_____

How do you feel about your own parenting?

_____

_____

_____

Traits and skills

Assignment 8.3a

What traits and skills do you have?

Look again at Figure 8. Now focus on what you wrote down in your own field. If done properly, it shows what you will do differently, which will make your children feel less caught in the middle.

When doing this, I apply the following skills:

- _____
- _____
- _____
- _____

Assignment 8.3b

Applied with success

Choose one skill or trait and write it down below.

_____

_____

_____

Suppose you have chosen the trait 'patience.' Then think when you managed to be patient. Maybe when waiting for the results of an exam, or when taking care of a sick child. The example does not have to involve the other parent. Below, briefly describe a number of situations that you remember.

_____

_____

_____

_____

_____

Assignment 8.3c

How do these skills help you to get on with your life? As a parent, as an ex, for yourself?

Two examples

> In order to respond well to the wish of the children that we are nice to each other as parents, I need the trait 'to endure.' I already used this trait or skill when I broke my leg and couldn't go on a skiing holiday. I learned that from my grandmother who was in a wheelchair and could not do much.
>
> In order to respond well to the children's message that they no longer want to go to their mother, I need the trait 'firmness.' I already used this trait or skill when I was a child and had to convince my parents that I did not want to study medicine and I inherited it from my father's relatives who were in the resistance during the war.

In the latter example, 'firmness' does not mean 'not letting the child go to his mother anymore,' but it is meant in terms of seeking a solution and a way of reacting that will allow space for the child to go to the other parent. Again, you have no control over the other parent (see pages XX and XX), and there is a risk that the children will grow up in a black-and-white world (see page XX). And because it is almost always better for the development of the children to spend time with both parents, parents better stand firm in this respect. Just like children who hate school usually go to school anyway, because it is important for their development, and just like going to the dentist, a lot of children do not want that either.

Assignment 8.3d

In the coming period, try experimenting in practice with traits or skills like those mentioned earlier in this section. Stress in children will decrease considerably as soon as one of the parents changes his or her behaviour. Imagine what your children will notice or start to feel if you start showing this different behaviour. Discuss all this with your network, and ask for help and support where you can use it.

Assignment 8.3e

Did you manage to put your resolution into action?

- Did you manage to apply that trait or skill?
- What made you succeed/fail?
- Do you think your children have noticed?
- Have you seen a reaction in them?

Write it down below.

_____

_____

_____

_____

_____

_____

_____

_____

GROUP THERAPY FOR HIGH-CONFLICT DIVORCE

After the eighth group meeting

The group treatment has ended. You did it. It has not been easy. You worked hard to get greater peace and quiet for your children and for all of you. That deserves congratulations. Changing is one of the most difficult tasks there are. Maybe you have been able to take big steps, maybe small ones. These small steps make a big difference in the long run.

An avid sailor once said that a change of course of a few degrees makes little difference the first few miles. But in the end you will end up in a completely different harbour.

In the project and in this workbook, we have often mentioned that you cannot change the other person. The thing is that you can do something yourself to reduce stress and tension in your child. You may not be 100 percent successful, but you have a significant influence on it.

To remember:

- Continue to recognise, stop and change the destructive patterns.

- Focus on your own life and your own pleasure, also when you are together with your children and friends.

- Check out the website of Villa Pinedo (www.villapinedo.nl) regularly and be inspired by it.

- Continue to pay attention to your own vulnerabilities and those of the other. Try to avoid escalations and be nice, even if it takes some effort.

- All children say they wish their parents treat each other 'normally.' Think about what they mean by this.

- Practise letting go and accepting.

- Believe that things can go differently.

- Ask people around you for support and the strength to persevere. And explain to them how they can support you in a way that is beneficial for the children.

- Look through your child's eyes and let that guide your actions.

Drawing 1 Dylan

Drawing 2 Masan

Drawing 3 Ruby

GROUP THERAPY FOR HIGH-CONFLICT DIVORCE

To conclude

Many children who participated in No Kids in the Middle, together with their parents, have actually been able to get (somewhat) out of the middle. Below are a few stories of parents and children in which they explain how stopping the deconstructive patterns has changed their lives.

> **Makar, father of Jaral**: I woke up with stress and went to bed with it. It's like in everything. I could hardly think of anything else and I could talk about little else. Now that we have both stopped fighting, I feel lighter, freer. I can be busy with other things again. The feeling that something negative can happen at any moment is gone. And Jaral is much more relaxed. That's plain to see.

> **Carol, mother of Eton and Jeremy**: During the evaluation, she says: 'Actually, after the first group meeting, we already made a move.' She looks at Sam, father of the children, sitting next to her. 'We had enough of it. We also noticed that when we started to discuss issues in the group, we didn't really want to go back to difficult things at all. As if you have had it all and now only want to look ahead.' Sam nods and adds: 'You don't want to go back to it anymore. Never again.'

> **Maecy, Jullian's mother**: I had all kinds of physical complaints. I think I've seen the family doctor more in the past period than in the 35 years before. It was like crazy. And now that things have changed between us, I really have far fewer complaints. Friends tell me that I look very different. More relaxed and not so stern and angry anymore. I see it myself too. I really didn't expect things to change between us. Even until the sixth session. And, yet, it happened. That really is a miracle. And yes, the children, they are happiest of all. Except for the youngest one, who isn't doing very well at school yet, but we have agreed to have that examined.
>
> When asked how she is doing, Lilyanne (6 years old) says: 'Very well! My parents don't fight anymore.' When asked how this is possible, she says: 'They just hardly talk to each other anymore. Only when there is something very important, they talk to each other. Much better that way.'

Ronald (14): I told my mother that I want to see my father more often. At first I didn't want to, but now I do. She was fine with it and called my father. Later she handed me the phone and my father and I agreed how we would do that. That goes well now and my mum is also relaxed about it. Actually, it feels normal again.

Michelle (10 years old): My parents say hello to each other again and have a short chat at the door. I don't think they really will be friends, but this is much better. I used to stand nearby because I was afraid they would start a fight or something, but now I can just go inside. Everything goes fine now.

Appendices

Appendix 1

Growing up in a black-and-white world

When children often experience that disagreements between parents result in increasing tensions, quarrels, demonising or a break in contact, they take that as an example for the rest of their lives.

Demonising means that you cannot see the good in the other parent anymore. For example, you become convinced that the other parent only wants to frustrate you. This never just comes out of the blue. It is often the result of painful, hurtful or sometimes frightening experiences. And all your attempts to change this have come to nothing. Beautiful moments you once shared disappear more and more in the background and with the best will in the world, you can no longer think of positive things about the other parent. If you ask the people in your network, they often cannot mention anything, either. This strengthens your idea that the other parent is no good at all.

We are not talking about situations of serious physical or sexual abuse, or about parents who are obviously incompetent as parents. As mentioned earlier, we only work with parents who both show good enough parenting.

Why is it so damaging for a child to grow up in a black-and-white world?

A child whose two most important people in his life cannot say anything positive about each other grows up in a world in which he does not learn to nuance. Someone is good or someone is bad. Someone is for or against me. Children learn to think in black and white instead of in colour shades. They do not learn to be flexible towards others. If someone else doesn't do something right, it means that the other person is not good. This can make it difficult for the child to enter into relationships at a later age, because the child has not learned to accept or tolerate that people also have not-so-good qualities and make mistakes.

When these children come of age, we often see the same mechanisms become active as the ones they saw during the conflicts between their parents. A partner is either right or wrong. Friends are for or against you. Partners or friends who make mistakes or say something nasty are wiped out. The danger is that these children will not be able to make deep connections in which sun and shade go hand in hand. Experience shows that children who grow up in such a situation run an increased risk of breaks in relationships.

There are also children who see all the good in one parent and all the bad in the other parent. They no longer want to have contact with the 'bad' parent. These children express themselves very negatively about one of the parents and, in doing so, they add fuel to the fire of the conflict cycles. One parent blames the other for having started it all. The other parent blames the other for turning the child against him or her.

In these situations, it is even more important to be able to see and name positive sides of each other again. A father, whose daughter no longer wanted to have anything to do with her mother, said that his daughter reacted furiously at first when he said something positive about her mother. As if she couldn't figure him out and would suddenly start to think differently about her mother. It made him despair, and he called his action 'a drop in the ocean.' Yet these drops prove to be invaluable. Together they form the meltwater that is needed to revive frozen and stuck relationships. Relationships between children and parents, but also future relationships of the children themselves.

Parents who are convinced that it is important for the development of their children that they see both parents, even if the situation is not ideal, manage to motivate their children, just as they manage to get their child to go to the dentist, or to school.

Is it any use when one of the parents is able to see positive things in the other parent, but the other parent isn't? The answer is yes. Of course it is better if both parents are able to do so. But even if only one parent can do it, it is of great value. After all, this way the child will learn that there is colour between black and white. It will learn to nuance. In this way, the child learns one thing from one parent and something else from the other. So keep it up! You can really make a difference for your child. Every parent wants his or her child to have loving relationships later in life. If necessary, ask for help from people from your network

Reconcile and forgive

Between black and white there is no grey, but a multitude of colours. This multitude of colours means that you acknowledge your own pain, that you feel how much you have been hurt by the other – how much you feel betrayed – but that you are still willing to reconcile with yourself. This is necessary if you want to go on with your life. This is also called 'mourning for the lost relationship.' Dealing with loss is difficult, not only the loss of a relationship, but also the loss of your dreams, how you wanted or expected it to be. You may find it very painful that your children have to go through the separation of their parents. There is a lot to deal with.

Maybe you regret certain choices you have made or things you have done. In that case, it is also important to forgive yourself. Sometimes that is even more difficult than forgiving someone else. Nobody, including yourself, can do everything right. You are not only black or white, but multicoloured. When you manage to reconcile with yourself and others, you will notice that there will be more 'air' and that you will be better able to get on with your life. The children will feel that, too, and be happy with it. And then you can be thankful again that the other person came into your life. Otherwise, you would never have had those wonderful children.

And how do you do that?

There are several ways to do this. We work on it in the No Kids in the Middle programme. Some parents benefit from yoga and meditation, others from a good conversation with a friend, still others are inspired by music and lyrics. Some are so tired of the conflicts and the energy and money it costs that they decide to try a different approach, and they can. And it is always the children who are at the centre. They are still at the beginning of their lives and are worth taking steps that you might not have taken without them.

Appendix 2

Growing up in a world full of stress

Children react differently to the years of tension and discord between their parents or guardians. But they all suffer from stress.

Young children are dependent on their parents, but parents are also important for older children. If the parents regularly argue, this is a source of tension for the child. It feels danger and gets stress. Usually, a child needs the help of parents to regulate stress. But if those parents are the source of the stress, the child often does not get enough help.

When children frequently experience tension, their bodies 'register' danger and become alarmed. Their bodies adjust to (perceiving) tensions and develop an increasingly sensitive antenna for this. The child watches whether new tensions arise, for instance by paying close attention to the intonation of voices, exchanged looks or the attitude of the parents. These children are, so to speak, always prepared for tensions and fights between the parents. Their bodies get ready to flee or to fight. Unfortunately, young children are often unable to flee or fight. And then they freeze. They feel paralysed and frozen and wait for it to pass (see also 'Escalation and de-escalation' on page 45 and 'Escalating conflicts, window of tolerance, trauma and de-escalation' on page 48). Some children start to feel responsible for stopping the conflict and try to help the parents or one of the parents. But if they don't succeed, they may feel guilty.

Some children, especially when they are a little older, close themselves off and focus as much as possible on other things, such as school, sports and friends. Sometimes they find a second home with neighbours or parents of their friends, also to avoid being an extra source of conflict for their parents. Apparently, nothing seems wrong with these children, but internally they often feel lonely, and stress does play a role.

Many children of divorced parents who argue a lot develop symptoms such as sleeping problems, anxiety, restless behaviour and avoidance behaviour. They say that they worry a lot and therefore have trouble sleeping. They are often tired. Their heads feel very full. Some of them have physical symptoms such as abdominal pain and headaches. Other children find it difficult to talk about or with the parents and avoid it. They say it is not too bad, or they deny the problems. They have experienced personally that they cannot speak freely because everything they say can be used in the conflict between the parents. Many children are very restless, have difficulty concentrating and, as a result, develop learning problems. Some have problems expressing emotions. Sometimes they show this in a very violent way, for instance by suddenly becoming very angry or sad. There are also children who barely show their emotions. Or they are insufficiently aware of it. A 12-year-old boy said: 'I don't really feel anything when I think about my parents.'

Some children are very reserved or shy in expressing their feelings. They seem insecure about whether or not their feelings deserve being acknowledged. Or they are afraid that if they express themselves, this may lead to tensions between the parents and further increase the stress.

Children who are always considerate of the tensions of parents also learn from that. They develop sensitivity to how the other person is doing. How the atmosphere in a relationship is, how the mood is. They always try to align with the other person in order to keep the atmosphere good so that no conflicts arise. The downside of this is that they forget to think about what they need themselves, or what their own boundaries are. They also notice this in the relationships they enter into.

Appendix 3

Separating and letting go

The change from joint parenthood to single parenthood is a transition. Everything has to be reorganised. Sometimes this leads to a lot of conflicts, and that makes it more and more difficult to become separated. People often say: 'you divorce as partners but you remain parents together.' This is only partly true, because you also have to get used to single parenthood.

As long as you have a lot of conflicts together, you keep being involved with each other and you don't really get separated. This is comparable to the transition process that migrants go through. First they leave their homes and have to let go of what was familiar, which is a difficult and painful process. Then they set off for a new situation. This transitional period (liminal phase) is often difficult, frightening and problematic. Nothing feels familiar anymore; there is nothing to go by. Often there is hope for better times, but as long as these times have not arrived, uncertainty and tension will prevail. Then symptoms may occur, such as sleeping problems, gloominess, outbursts of anger and confusion. When they arrive in the new situation, a country where they are allowed to stay and work, then they can find something to hold on to and calm down.

This is the same with a divorce. The old does not work anymore, and the new does not work yet. Parents can remain stuck in the liminal phase, the transition between the old family and the new life. As long as parents are trying to influence and change the other person, a lot of often-negative energy goes into these efforts. Then, parents are not really divorced.

Conflict divorces are divorces that have not yet succeeded. When parents let go of each other and focus more on their own lives, they really get divorced. Then they are no longer so involved with each other. This will allow for more positive energy in their own lives and those of the children and the important people around them.

Voices of parents

> **Sylvana**: I cursed my ex and I could have kicked myself for having children with this man. In the group, I also got really irritated by him. Until the moment I understood that there is nothing I can do to change him. I can only try to do the best I can myself. That has changed a lot.

Rodger: I have come to realise that you shouldn't look at the other person as your ex, but as the other parent. That helped me. Or rather . . . that helped my children.

Nigel: I have come to see that I cannot cut Mirjam from my life. No matter how hard I have tried. She is the mother of our children and she will continue to do things I do not agree with. She will continue to send messages which I need like a hole in the head. I will just have to endure that. And the crazy thing is, it actually makes me feel like a better parent.

Dione: Letting go, that's what I found and still find the most difficult thing. I still don't always manage. Letting go of how things go at the other's place, or rather, how they don't go. They really deserve a different kind of father. But that can't be changed. And I have to accept that. So difficult . . .

Appendix 4

Experiences of parents from practice

Everyone sometimes faces situations in which you just don't know how to react – situations in which you tend to fall back into old patterns.

In this appendix, we give an anthology of situations that parents have shared with us. The answers they found may be helpful to you. The examples may not always be the correct answer to the dilemmas described. But they are examples of parents who have searched for a way to react that spares the child.

The other person does not stick to the agreements

A father who sees that his children become very restless and busy when their mother does not pick them up at the agreed time repeatedly tries to make agreements about this. Sometimes the children are not picked up, and then they get worried. Mother often cannot be reached. Discussions with the mother about this invariably end in an argument. Father decides to approach it in a different way.

He explains to his children that he is sure that mum wants to see them but that she is sometimes a bit forgetful, just as he often forgets to put his bicycle inside (which has already been stolen three times). He reassures his children that he is sure that nothing serious has happened and that they are allowed to game for another while.

The outcome remains the same. Sometimes the children are picked up too late or not at all. But because it no longer leads to fights between them as parents, the children stay calm. Besides, mother now sometimes calls to say that she will come a little later. After all, she no longer needs to expect any accusations.

If you are worried as a parent

A mother says she is very worried about her 12-year-old son. He has just started in first year and is chaos itself. You have to remind him of everything. Often, he doesn't even know if he has any homework or he leaves important books at school.

Her worries grow when she finds out that father does nothing to get their son to do his homework. When she asks what he has done, he tells her that he can game most of the time and that his father regularly goes into town with his new girlfriend while he stays at home. Mother finds it unbelievable. Whining that you want to see your child more and then not being home and leaving him to his fate. She talks to the father about this, but it does not do any good. Sometimes it seems to help for a while, but most of the time things are back to square one after a week.

Mother discusses this with her son and asks him if he wants to make it through the year, and what he himself thinks he needs. They get into a conversation where the son says he wants to decide for himself. They agree that it is okay for now, but that after the Christmas report they will see how he is doing and whether new agreements need to be made, and if so, if they will involve school. By Christmas, things so not look promising. They agree with school that he will get a homework tutor. Father is fine with that.

References

Lawick, M.J. van (2014). Geweld. In A. Savenije, M.J. van Lawick & E.T.M. Reijmers (ed.), *Handboek Systeemtherapie*. Utrecht: de Tijdstroom, pp. 659–672.

Scheinkman, M. & Fishbane, M.D. (2007). De kwetsbaarheidscyclus: Werken met impasses in parentherapie. *Gezinstherapie Wereldwijd*, *18*(3), 241–271.

Visser, M., Finkenauer, C., Schoemaker, K., Kluwer, E., Rijken, R. van der, Lawick, J. van, Bom, H., Schipper, J.C. de & Lamers-Winkelman, F. (2017). I'll never forgive you: High conflict divorce, social network, and co-parenting conflicts. *Journal of Child and Family Therapy*, *26*(3), 3055–3066. JCFS-D-16–00013R2.

Visser, M. & van Lawick, J. (2021). *Group Therapy for High-Conflict Divorce: The 'No Kids in the Middle' Intervention Programme*. Routledge.